M. Tuench

Victorious Eschatology

Harold R. Eberle
&
Martin Trench

WORLDCAST PUBLISHING
YAKIMA, WASHINGTON

Victorious Eschatology
by Harold R. Eberle and Martin Trench

Worldcast Publishing
P.O. Box 10653
Yakima, WA 98909-1653
(509) 248-5837
www.worldcastpublishing.com
office@worldcastpublishing.com

ISBN 978-1-882523-31-8
Cover by Paul Jones

What Others Are Saying

When I first read *Victorious Eschatology* a light bulb went on in a dim part of my brain! Since I have become a strong advocate of dominion theology, I have realized that my previous Scofield Bible eschatology would no longer cut it. However, while I knew what I wasn't, I didn't quite know what I was until Harold Eberle and Martin Trench came along. This is one of the most important books I have read in a long time!

C. Peter Wagner, Presiding Apostle
International Coalition of Apostles

I cannot imagine getting up every morning with a defeatist attitude about life. Nor can I imagine serving a God who cannot overcome evil, but simply snatches away a few poor souls. Harold Eberle and Martin Trench's new book, *Victorious Eschatology*, gives us a clear understanding of what to expect as kings of the King.

Don Atkins
President Kingdom Quest Ministries

Victorious Eschatology is one of the most interesting books that I have recently read! I do not know Martin Trench but I do know Harold Eberle. Harold has always been radical in his pursuit of God—His times and His purposes. This book by Eberle and Trench will cause you to ask many questions and rethink many of the doctrines that captured you in the past. If you have never held certain views on the rapture, or if you have never read the book of Daniel, or thought much about the end-times, I believe this book will challenge and give you fresh insight as you relate it to Scripture. Yes, this book pushes you to the edge! But in reality, I think that is where we will find ourselves in the days ahead!

Chuck Pierce
President, Glory of Zion International, Inc.

Credits and Thanks

We have drawn from the writings of numerous authors whose names and works are mentioned in the bibliography of this book. They have done research from which we benefited and hope to bless you.

Pastors Mike and Ruth Lightfoot deserve a special thank you for their input and encouragement. Pastor Ted Hansen is a pioneer in Christian thought and he has been a constant inspiration. We also need to thank the thousands of Christians who listened to us teach these truths while we still were studying and developing our own understanding of the Church rising in victory and power before the return of Jesus Christ.

James Bryson is our hardest and most critical editor. Tristan Kohl is brilliant and amazing at finding mistakes no one else can see. Annette Bradley is the expert and our final editor.

Thanks to all of you.

Table of Contents

Foreword

Read this book with the help of the Holy Spirit. Do not approach it with religious or denominational filters, but allow the Holy Spirit to witness truth to you. What Harold Eberle and Martin Trench have written here will cause a shift in your thinking of eschatology or endtime events. We need a shift that will move the Church from a rapture mentality to a harvest theology. We must take off the grave clothes and put on the wedding gown as the Bride of Christ. We are the Bride of Christ and the Groom is coming for His Bride, but He is coming for a Bride in victory that is bringing the Kingdom of God on the Earth by fulfilling the will of the Father.

We are not the Church in failure running out the back door while the devil kicks in the front door. We are the Church of Luke 10:19 that has authority over *all* the power of the enemy.

One thing that I have noticed is that Christians who focus on the harvest don't really have much time to worry about a rapture. Their goal is to get as many people into the Kingdom as possible in preparation for the wedding. A victorious eschatology will put a rapture mindset behind and a harvest work before you.

Cal Pierce
Director Healing Rooms Ministries International

Introduction

The greatest revival the world has ever seen is ahead of us. The greatest men and women of God to walk the Earth will walk it in the coming years. Before Jesus returns, the Church will rise in glory, unity, and maturity. The Kingdom of God will grow and advance until it fills the Earth.

Most of the great leaders throughout Church history held such a victorious, optimistic view. It was not until the Twentieth Century that Christians became more skeptical and pessimistic. During World War I, Christians in Europe began embracing a negative view. Christians in North America followed suit during the Depression, followed by World War II. As the world was thrust face to face with challenges and the wickedness of war, people embraced a negative view of humanity and a pessimistic view of the future.

It was during those periods when many Christians embraced an eschatology of defeat. They came to believe that the world gradually is slipping under the influence of wicked leaders, and, eventually, the devil will control the economic and religious systems of the world. Preachers who embraced that pessimistic view became more and more focused on a coming Great Tribulation in which God would destroy the Earth. Much teaching focused on an antichrist figure taking over this world. Negative views of the future snowballed and grew more negative, climaxing at the turn of the millennium with a great expectation that God was about to end the world as we know it.

We will refer to that negative view as the *popular*

endtime view, because it became the most commonly held view during the last part of the Twentieth Century.

Now that we have crossed into the new millennium, Christians are lifting their eyes to the future. Many leaders are discovering that the Scriptures give us a more optimistic view than they previously had believed. They are embracing a *victorious eschatology*, which teaches that Jesus Christ and His Church are going to take over this world, not Satan.

In the following pages we will be contrasting *victorious eschatology* with the *popular endtime view*.

As pastors, we (Harold Eberle and Martin Trench) use to believe and teach the popular endtime view. However, even as we taught our church congregations the related ideas, we both realized that there are many Scriptures which simply do not fit into the scenario of events proposed by the popular endtime view. After several years of in-depth study, we have come to believe that *victorious eschatology* is more true to the Scriptures.

As we present a victorious eschatology to you in the pages which follow, we will insert a few quotes from well-known preachers, teachers, and reformers which show how the fathers of the faith shared a victorious eschatology. Not every leader throughout Church history would explain every verse of the Bible the same as we will; however, the fundamental view that the Church will rise in victory and power before the return of Jesus Christ has been the predominant view of the Church for the last 2,000 years.

As we study the Word of God together and you read the corresponding quotations, we hope your faith will rise to a level fitting a child of the King.

John Wesley
All unprejudiced persons may see with their eyes, that he [God] is already renewing the face of the earth: And we have strong reason to hope that the work he hath begun he will carry on unto the day of the Lord Jesus; that he will never intermit this blessed work of his Spirit until he has fulfilled all his promises, until he hath put a period to sin and misery, and infirmity, and death; and re-established universal holiness and happiness, and caused all the inhabitants of the earth to sing together "Hallelujah."
(*The Works of John Wesley*, 1985: 499)

Jonathan Edwards
The visible kingdom of Satan shall be overthrown, and the kingdom of Christ set up on the ruins of it, everywhere throughout the whole habitable globe.
(*The Works of Jonathan Edwards*, 1974: 488)

Charles H. Spurgeon
I myself believe that King Jesus will reign, and the idols be utterly abolished; but I expect the same power which turned the world upside down once, will still continue to do it. The Holy Ghost would never suffer the imputation to rest upon His holy name that He was not able to convert the world.
(*Life and Work of Charles Haddon Spurgeon*, 1992 (4):210)

I. Understanding Matthew 24

In this section we will study Matthew 24, a passage which has become known as the "Olivet Discourse" because Jesus gave this teaching to His disciples while they were gathered on the Mount of Olives. We will begin in Matthew 24:3, where the disciples asked Jesus some key questions.

As He was sitting on the Mount of Olives, the disciples came to Him privately, saying, "Tell us, when will these things happen, and what will be the sign of Your coming, and of the end of the age?"

In the verses that follow this one, our Lord gave answers which we will be examining. How you understand His answers determines what you believe about the endtimes, the tribulation, the antichrist, and the unfolding of all future events.

Introduction to Matthew 24

After the disciples asked Jesus their questions in Matthew 24:3, Jesus answered talking about false leaders claiming to be Christ, wars, earthquakes, famines, persecutions, and people falling away from the faith. He also talked about the gospel being preached around the world, followed by destruction, tribulation, and people being taken away.

Christians who believe the popular endtime view study our Lord's answers and conclude that all of the events listed are going to happen in the future, shortly before the end of the world.

Victorious eschatology comes to very different conclusions when studying Matthew 24. We will go with you through Matthew 24 verse by verse to explain, but first we need to identify clearly the questions Jesus was asked by His disciples.

As He was sitting on the Mount of Olives, the disciples came to Him privately, saying, "Tell us, when will these things happen, and what will be the sign of Your coming, and of the end of the age?"
(Matt. 24:3)

Some translations (*e.g. King James Version*) end this verse with "end of the world," because the word *aion*, which is used in the original Greek, may be translated as "age" or "world." Using the term "world," popular endtime teachers tend to summarize

7

the questions asked by the disciples into an inquiry about the second coming of Jesus and the end of the world. Therefore, when Jesus gives His answer in the verses that follow, all His comments are thought to be answering that question.

Victorious eschatology begins by noting that in Matthew 24:3, the disciples asked Jesus not just one question, but three questions.

Question #1: *"When will these things happen?"*
Question #2: *"What will be the sign of Your coming?"*
Question #3: *"What about the end of the age (world)?"*

Recognizing three distinct questions dramatically changes how we understand the answers Jesus gives in the verses to follow. We will see how our Lord first answers question number one in Matthew 24:4-28. Then He answers the second question in Matthew 24:29-34. Finally, He answers the question about the end of the age (or the end of the world) in Matthew 24:35-25:46.

Question #1: "When Will These Things Happen?"

The first question asked of Jesus was, "When will these things happen?" Before we look at Jesus' answer, we need to identify what are "these things" about which the disciples were asking.

Christians who have been taught the popular end-time view immediately think "these things" refers to the events which will precede the second coming of Jesus and the end of the world. We will come to a very different understanding if we read the context of this Bible passage.

Matthew 23 tells us about a day when Jesus was speaking in the temple in Jerusalem. First, He warned the crowds and His disciples to watch out for the scribes and Pharisees (23:2-12). Then beginning in Matthew 23:13, Jesus turned from the disciples and directed His words directly toward those religious leaders. We can sense the flavor of His message by glancing at the first few words of each verse that follows:

verse 13:
"But woe to you, scribes and Pharisees, hypocrites..."
verse 14:
"Woe to you, scribes and Pharisees, hypocrites..."
verse 15:
"Woe to you, scribes and Pharisees, hypocrites..."
verse 16:
"Woe to you, blind guides..."

9

Jesus was rebuking the religious leaders right there in their temple. Glance down a few verses and pick up the intensity of His rebuke:

verse 23:
"Woe to you, scribes and Pharisees, hypocrites!..."
verse 24:
"You blind guides..."
verse 25:
"Woe to you, scribes and Pharisees, hypocrites!..."
verse 26:
"You blind Pharisee..."
verse 27:
"Woe to you, scribes and Pharisees, hypocrites!..."
verse 29:
"Woe to you, scribes and Pharisees, hypocrites!..."

Jesus built up to a climax in which He declared a severe judgment against those religious leaders.

"You serpents, you brood of vipers, how will you escape the sentence of hell? Therefore, behold, I am sending you prophets and wise men and scribes; some of them you will kill and crucify, and some of them you will scourge in your synagogues, and persecute from city to city, so that upon you may fall the guilt of all righteous blood shed on earth, from the blood of righteous Abel to the blood of Zechariah, the son of Berechiah, whom you murdered between the temple and

the altar. Truly I say to you, all these
things shall come upon this generation."
(Matt. 23:33-36)

At that moment, you wouldn't have wanted to be sitting with the scribes and Pharisees.

As Jesus declared coming judgment, He referred to the blood of every righteous person, from Abel to Zechariah. That is significant because in the Hebrew Bible, Abel is in the first book and Zechariah is in the last book. Therefore, Jesus was saying to the religious leaders that the guilt of the blood of every righteous person—from the beginning of their Holy Book to the end—will come upon them and on their generation!

Judgment had been decreed!

Typically, we understand a generation to be 40 years in length (*i.e.,* the Hebrew people wandered in the wilderness for 40 years until a generation passed away). So if Jesus' words were to come true literally, then we should expect the judgment He declared to fall upon those religious leaders who were listening to His words and to those who would be around during the following 40 years.

In Matthew 23, Jesus went on to tell more specifically how this great judgment was to occur. In verses 37 and 38, He cried out:

"Jerusalem, Jerusalem, who kills the
prophets and stones those who are sent to
her! How often I wanted to gather your
children together, the way a hen gathers
her chicks under her wings, and you were

11

unwilling. Behold, your house is being left to you desolate!"

Jesus declared these words while standing in the temple in Jerusalem. He cried out to the scribes and Pharisees saying destruction would come upon them, their city, and their temple.

The Judgment Fulfilled in 70 AD

Did the words of Jesus come true? Well, they would have had to have been fulfilled by 70 AD, because Jesus made His declaration around 30 AD. Historically, did anything happen? Yes, in 70 AD Jerusalem was destroyed. Within 40 years after Jesus declared judgment, 20,000 Roman soldiers, under the command of General Titus, surrounded the city and cut off all supplies of food for four months so the people would starve. Then they came into the city and mercilessly killed over one million Jews. The soldiers set the temple on fire, and they led away 97,000 Jews as captives.*

At that time the Jewish population was decimated. Historically, little is known about the Jews' actions or lives for the following 60 years. It was not until 130 AD that they began reassembling with enough strength to attempt one last rebellion against Rome. Then after three years of battling, the Romans were able to crush that rebellion, and Israel no more was recognized as a nation (until 1948). It also was at

---

* Flavius Josephus, *The War of the Jews*, vi:ix:3.

that time that the Roman commander ordered the temple in Jerusalem to be demolished so completely, that each and every stone was carried away, and then the land upon which the temple had stood was ploughed over completely. The temple was destroyed totally, as Jesus said it would be.*

Historians have a good number of documents from that time period which give us information about the destruction of the temple and Jerusalem. However, most of our information comes from Josephus, a Jewish historian who lived at that time and was an eye witness of the events. Concerning the war against and destruction of Jerusalem, Josephus wrote many things, including the following:

> ...when they [the Roman soldiers] were come to the houses to plunder them, they found in them entire families of dead men...that is of such as died by the famine; they then stood in a horror at this sight, and went out without touching anything. But although they had this commiseration for such as were destroyed in that manner, yet had they not the same for those that were still alive, but they ran every one through whom they met with, and obstructed the very lanes with their dead bodies, and made the whole city run with blood, to such a degree indeed that the fire of many of

* The Wailing Wall in Jerusalem today was never a part of the temple which existed in Jesus' day.

the houses was quenched with these
men's blood.   (vi:viii:5)

It is worth reading the whole of Josephus' writings about the fall of Jerusalem. What is so astounding about them is how clearly—sometimes word for word—they fulfilled the prophecy of Jesus in Matthew 23-24. The writings of Josephus are available in most Christian bookshops or libraries, and can be accessed freely on many websites.

John Wesley
This was most punctually fulfilled: for after the temple was burned, Titus, the Roman general, ordered the very foundations of it to be dug up; after which the ground on which it stood was ploughed by Turnus Rufus...*this generation* of men now living *shall not pass till all these things be done*—The expression implies that a great part of that generation would be passed away, but not the whole. Just so it was; for the city and temple were destroyed thirty-nine or forty years after. (*The Works of John Wesley*, 1985)

Eusebius
All this occurred in this manner, in the second year of the reign of Vespasian [70 AD], according to the predictions of our Lord and Saviour, Jesus Christ. (*Ecclesiastical History*, III:7)

The Context of Matthew 24

We will discuss the destruction of Jerusalem and the temple more fully later, but here we are noting the context in which Matthew 24 begins.

We know that in the original Greek manuscripts of the New Testament there are no chapter breaks. Matthew 23 flows right into Matthew 24 with no interruption. Matthew 24:1 goes on to say:

> *Jesus came out from the temple and was going away when His disciples came up to point out the temple buildings to Him. And He said to them, "Do you not see all of these things? Truly I say to you, not one stone here will be left upon another, which will not be torn down."*
>
> (Matt. 24:1-2)

After repeating that the temple would be demolished completely, Jesus walked away from the temple with His disciples.

Then the next verse starts off saying,

> *As He was sitting on the Mount of Olives....* (Matt. 24:3)

Where is the Mount of Olives? It is the hill just outside of the temple in Jerusalem. As Jesus sat down with His disciples they most likely were looking right at the temple from which they just had exited.

Put yourself in the disciples' shoes. If you had been sitting there with Jesus, what would you ask? On the forefront of the disciples' minds was the judgment which Jesus just had decreed over Jerusalem and the temple. The disciples asked:

"Tell us, when will these things happen?"

They were asking, "When will Jerusalem and the temple be destroyed?"

As we mentioned earlier, popular endtime teachers assume that the disciples were asking about the end of the world. It is not until the third question that they asked Jesus about the end. The reason that they asked about the end at the same time that they asked about the temple being destroyed was because in their Jewish minds what Jesus just had predicted was so cataclysmic that they must have wondered if it would be the end of the world. They were shocked at the thought of God's holy temple being destroyed. How could life go on without it? Could it possibly coincide with the end of the world? If not, when would that occur?

We will examine our Lord's answers to the second and third questions, later. But here, we need to realize that the first question the disciples asked Jesus is, "When will these things—Jerusalem and the temple—be destroyed?"

Within a Generation

As we go on to study our Lord's answers, keep in mind His time frame. Jesus said Jerusalem and the temple would be destroyed within a generation. He repeated that time frame in Matthew 24:34, saying:

> *"Truly I say to you, this generation will not pass away until all these things take place."*

Can we accept these words of Jesus literally? Yes! Popular endtime teaching sees all of the events of which Jesus prophesied in Matthew 24 happening not by 70 AD, but 2,000 years later, in our future. Therefore, they cannot accept the time frame of that generation which Jesus declared in two separate passages (Matt. 23:36 and 24:34). Some popular endtime teachers will explain their position by redefining the word "generation" to mean "race," and hence, they can say that the race of Jewish people will not pass away before the end of the world. Others claim that the generation about which Jesus was talking was the generation which would see all of the endtime events listed in Matthew 24:4-33—that generation will not pass away until Jesus returns.

We believe that Jesus knew exactly about what He was speaking. **Everything that is prophesied between Matthew 23:36 and Matthew 24:34 took place exactly as Jesus declared, during the generation which was alive when Jesus declared those words.** This is what we will show you in the following pages.

> **Origen of Alexandria**
> I challenge anyone to prove my statement untrue if
> I say that the entire Jewish nation was destroyed
> less than one whole generation later on account of
> these sufferings which they inflicted on Jesus. For it
> was, I believe, forty-two years from the time when
> they crucified Jesus to the destruction of Jerusalem.
> (*Against Celsus*, IV:XXII)

Jesus Answers the First Question

Jesus gives His answer to the first question in Matthew 24:4-22. We will examine His answer verse by verse.

Matthew 24:4-5: Many Claiming to be Christ

"See to it that no one misleads you. For many will come in My name, saying, 'I am the Christ,' and will mislead many."

Christians who have heard only the popular end-time view immediately place these words of Jesus in the future, shortly before the end of the world. They are looking for some evil leader or several leaders in our lifetime to start claiming that they are the Christ.

That is the first error we need to correct. Jesus was answering the question concerning when Jerusalem and the temple would be destroyed. That event happened in 70 AD, within 40 years of the time in which Jesus prophesied it. Jesus told His disciples that soon many people would come claiming to be the Christ. For Jesus' words to be fulfilled, those imposters would have had to come in the First Century of the Church.

Did that happen historically? Yes. Right after the death of Jesus, many leaders rose capturing the hearts of the Jewish people. That may seem difficult for us to understand today, but we need to keep in mind the culture of that day. The Jewish people were desperately looking for a Messiah, someone to free them from Roman domination. Their hope and much of their religious system was based on a coming Messiah. When Jesus died, many of His followers gave up believing that He was the Messiah. Other leaders quickly arose, drawing large followings.

Eusebius
After the Lord was taken up into heaven the demons put forth a number of men who claimed to be gods. (*The History of the Church,* 1965)

St. Jerome
At the time of the Jewish captivity, there were many leaders who declared themselves to be Christs, so that while the Romans were actually besieging them, there were three factions within.
(Cited in: Thomas Aquinas' *Golden Chain,* 1956)

> **The Venerable Bede**
> For many came forward, when destruction was hanging over Jerusalem, saying that they were Christs.
> (Cited in: Thomas Aquinas' *Golden Chain*, 1956)

> **John Wesley**
> And, indeed, never did so many imposters appear in the world as a few years before the destruction of Jerusalem, undoubtedly because that was the time wherein the Jews in general expected the Messiah.
> (*The Works of John Wesley*, 1985)

Matthew 24:6-7: Wars and Rumors of War

"You will be hearing of wars and rumors of wars. See that you are not frightened, for those things must take place, but that is not yet the end. For nation will rise against nation, and kingdom against kingdom...."

Approximately 2,000 years ago when Jesus was sitting on the Mount of Olives with His disciples, He prophesied of coming wars. Interestingly, there were no signs of "wars and rumors of wars" when Jesus prophesied this. The power of Rome seemed to be stable, strong, irresistible, and permanent. Historically, the period was referred to as *Pax Romana*, that is,

"Roman Peace." Of course, the enemies of Rome would not have spoken of the time so graciously, but Rome definitely was established in that region of the world. It was at that time that Jesus prophesied of coming wars.

Did the prophecy of Jesus come true within that generation? Indeed, wars began to break out all over the empire. The Jews lived in constant fear, with 50,000 Jews being slain in Seleucia and 20,000 in Caesaria. Then in 66 AD, 50,000 Jews were killed in Alexandria. Within a period of 18 months, four emperors in Rome were murdered violently. Civil war broke out in the city of Rome. It was a time of great turmoil and there were constant rumors of new rebellions.

Matthew 24:7: Famines

"...in various places there will be famines...."

Did famines and earthquakes occur during the generation of the disciples?

In Acts 11 we are told about the "great famine."

...Agabus stood up and began to indicate by the Spirit that there would certainly be a __great famine__ all over the world. And this took place in the reign of Claudius.
(Acts 11:28; underlining added)

That famine was so severe in the region of Judah that

21

we can read two places in the New Testament where Christians took offerings to collect money for believers suffering there (Acts 11:29-30; I Cor. 16:1-3).

The historian Josephus wrote about the devastation of that period:

> But the famine was too hard for all other passions, and it is destructive to nothing so much as to modesty...insomuch that children pulled the very morsels that their fathers were eating out of their very mouths, and what was still more to be pitied, so did the mothers do as to their infants; and when those that were most dear were perishing under their hands, they were not ashamed to take from them the very last drops that might preserve their lives...but the seditious everywhere came upon them immediately, and snatched away from them what they had gotten from others; for when they saw any house shut up, this was to them a signal that the people within had gotten some food; whereupon they broke open the doors, and ran in and took pieces of what they were eating, almost up out of their very throats, and this by force; the old men, who held their food fast, were beaten; and if the women hid what they had within their hands, their hair was torn for so doing; nor was there any commiseration shown either to the aged or to the infants, but

they lifted up children from the ground as they hung upon the morsels they had gotten, and shook them down upon the floor. (v:x:3)

Knowing about this famine and the destruction of Jerusalem to follow, we can see why Jesus said to the women of Jerusalem:

"Daughters of Jerusalem, stop weeping for Me, but weep for yourselves and for your children. For behold, the days are coming when they will say, 'Blessed are the barren, and the wombs that never bore, and the breasts that never nursed!'"
(Luke 23:28-29)

Eusebius
Under [Claudius] the world was visited with a famine, which writers that are entire strangers to our religion have recorded in their histories.
(*Ecclesiastical History*, II:8)

Matthew 24:7: Earthquakes

"...in various places there will be... earthquakes."

Not only did the Earth quake when Jesus died on the cross (Matt. 27:51-52) and again when He rose from the dead (Matt. 28:2), but history tells us that the few years just previous to the fall of Jerusalem in 70 AD was a time of unusually high seismic activity. The most famous earthquake was the destruction of Pompeii in 63 AD. The writers of the period also tell us about earthquakes at Crete, Smyrna, Miletus, Chios, Samos, Laodicea, Heirapolis, Campania, Colossae, Rome, and Judea.

Matthew 24:8: Birth Pangs

"But all these things are merely the beginning of birth pangs."

It is common today for people trained in the popular endtime view to look at present-day natural disasters and claim that they are signs of the imminent return of Jesus, yet that is *not* what Jesus said. He was very clear that these signs would happen within that generation, and furthermore, they would *not* be signs of the end of the world but *"merely the beginning of birth pangs."* These birth pangs were to precede the destruction of Jerusalem and the temple.

Matthew 24:9: Persecution

"Then they will deliver you to tribulation, and will kill you, and you will be hated by all nations because of My name."

First came the persecution instigated by the Jewish religious leaders. Saul was among those leaders who oversaw the men who were putting Christians to death. The book of Acts describes that persecution saying:

> *And on that day a great persecution began against the church in Jerusalem, and they were all scattered throughout the regions of Judea and Samaria, except the apostles.* (Acts 8:1b)

That *"great persecution"* continued to spread and soon government officials such as King Herod got involved (Acts 12:1).

The persecution became even more intense in the year 64 AD. That was the year when over one-third of the city of Rome burned to the ground. The significance of that event is difficult for modern people to grasp. If we compared it with the recent destruction of the Twin Towers in New York, we would have to say that the fire in Rome was far more devastating. Rome was considered the center of the civilized world during the First Century and over one-third of the city was destroyed. Nero, who was the Emperor at that time, blamed Christians for that terrible fire, and then he began what Church historians call "The Great Persecution." Not only were thousands of Christians tortured, but Nero actually had Christians covered in tar and then lit on fire so that the light given off would light up his gardens while he entertained guests there in the evenings.*

---

* Cornelius Tacitus, *Annals of Imperial Rome* (New York: Penguin Books, 1989), XV, 44.

Matthew 24:10-13: Apostasy and False Prophets

> *"At that time many will fall away and
> will betray one another and hate one an-
> other. Many false prophets will arise and
> will mislead many. Because lawlessness
> is increased, most people's love will grow
> cold. But the one who endures to the end,
> he will be saved."*

Soon after the death of our Lord, false prophets
began appearing on the scene. Several times Paul
warned his followers to watch out for the false prophets. John explained that during his lifetime *"...many
false prophets have gone out into the world"* (I John
4:1). Similarly, Peter warned, *"false prophets also
arose among the people, just as there will also be false
teachers among you, who will secretly introduce de-
structive heresies..."* (II Peter 2:1).

The first major group was the Judaizers who
taught that Gentiles had to become Jewish proselytes
and adhere to the Law of Moses, as well as have faith
in Christ.

Then came the Gnostics. History tells us that by
the year 150 AD, about one-third of all Christians
were involved in Gnosticism. To grasp the influence of
this heresy, imagine how it would be today if one-
third of all Christians in the world or in your own
community were taken in by a certain heretical teaching. That is exactly what happened during those early
days when the Church was struggling to survive.

Since our understanding of Gnosticism is key to

understanding the problems of the First-Century Church, it is worth taking a moment to explain.

Gnosticism in the First and Second Century

At the foundation of Gnosticism was a worldview in which the spiritual world was separated from the natural world in the minds of its followers. The spiritual world was considered good and the natural world was thought to be corrupt and evil. As certain leaders attempted to merge this worldview with Christianity, they concluded that God could not have taken on flesh nor come into this evil world in Jesus. This led to several false teachings about the nature of Jesus (which we discuss below). Thinking of this natural world as evil also led them to believe that a person must be very spirit-conscious to be a good Christian. Hence, they developed mystical understandings and taught that a person must have secret knowledge to know God. From this the word *Gnosticism* came, for it literally means "knowledge."

Gnosticism took many forms, but one of the most influential groups completely rejected the Old Testament. They declared that the God of the Old Testament was the devil and Jesus had come to reveal an "unknown Father" to us. Other Gnostics taught that the Old Testament rituals were still valid for Christians. Some were hyper-ascetic and taught vegetarianism and were opposed to any sexual expression— even within marriage, while others taught "freedom" from all laws and held orgies as part of their rituals.

One of the most prominent Gnostic teachers was a

man called Cerinthus. He was a Jew who lived in Asia Minor, teaching that Jesus was the son of Joseph and Mary (not born of a virgin)—an ordinary man. A heavenly spirit called "the Christ" came upon Jesus at his baptism and left him at the crucifixion. Jesus had brought secret teachings which would enable people to overcome enslavement to the physical world, but the Jewish customs also had to be observed. Those who proved faithful to these teachings and observances would live for a literal 1,000 years of sensual pleasures. These teachings of Cerinthus flourished throughout Asia Minor.

Knowing that Ephesus was in the region of Cerinthus' influence gives us insight into Paul's words when he warned the church elders in Ephesus of false teachers springing up around them:

> *I know that after my departure savage wolves will come in among you, not sparing the flock; and from among your own selves men will arise, speaking perverse things, to draw away the disciples after them.* (Acts 20:29-30)

Cerinthus claimed that he had received "another gospel" from an angel. In light of this, it is interesting to note what Paul wrote to the Galatians who were also in that region:

> *I am amazed that you are so quickly deserting Him who called you by the grace of Christ, for a different gospel; which is*

really not another; only there are some who are disturbing you and want to distort the gospel of Christ. But even if we, or an angel from heaven, should preach to you a gospel contrary to what we have preached to you, he is to be accursed!

(Gal. 1:6-8)

Historical records tell us that John was so horrified at Cerinthus' teachings that on one occasion when John walked into the public baths with his disciples at Ephesus, he saw Cerinthus, and so, John ran out of the bath-house warning his disciples that the house may fall down because "Cerinthus, the enemy of the truth, is within."*

It was to fight Gnosticism that John wrote his first two epistles. Knowing this helps us to understand his teachings. For example, I John starts with a declaration that is diametrically opposed to the Gnostic view of Jesus.

What was from the beginning, what we have heard, what we have seen with our eyes, what we have looked at and touched with our hands, concerning the Word of Life—and the life was manifested, and we have seen and testify and proclaim to you the eternal life, which was with the Father and was manifested to us.

(I John 1:1-2)

---

* Pamphilius Eusebius, *Ecclesiastical History* (New York: Harvard University Press, 1980), III, 28.

Do you see how profound this statement is? Because the Gnostics thought of the natural world as evil, they could not believe that Jesus could have been God and at the same time have taken on human flesh. Therefore, John started off his letter by declaring that he and the other apostles heard Jesus, saw Him, and touched Him with their hands. Jesus was God and He took on flesh. He manifested in this world.

John goes on in his letter dealing with one truth after another opposing the cult of Gnosticism. Toward the middle of his letter, John warns about the false prophets of Gnosticism.

> *Beloved, do not believe every spirit, but test the spirits to see whether they are from God, because many false prophets have gone out into the world. By this you know the Spirit of God: every spirit that confesses that Jesus Christ has come in the flesh is from God; and every spirit that does not confess Jesus is not from God; this is the spirit of the antichrist, of which you have heard that it is coming, and now it is already in the world.*
>
> (I John 4:1-3)

Knowing that John was addressing his letter to First-Century Christians who were being swept into Gnosticism by the thousands, we more easily can understand his warning to judge various teachers. The most fundamental basis for judging them, John declared, pertains to what they teach about Jesus

Christ. The true prophets and teachers will teach that Jesus has come in the flesh. The false will deny this and/or deny that Jesus is from God.

Not only do we get a glimpse here of the cultish tendencies infiltrating the early Church, but John also referred to the "antichrist," another topic which is key for our discussion of Matthew 24 and endtime events.

The Antichrist

When modern Christians hear the word "antichrist," the images which come into their minds are determined by whether they have been trained to believe the popular endtime view or victorious eschatology. Christians raised with the popular endtime view believe that shortly before Jesus returns to Earth, there will be an evil ruler, possessed by Satan, who will try to take over rulership of the world by taking control of the world's economic system and establishing a false religious system. That coming leader is referred to as the antichrist.

Is that image of the antichrist really in the Bible?

Actually, the word "antichrist" is mentioned only in four passages of the Bible. All four are in I and II John. We will look briefly at each of those passages to learn what the Bible actually says about the antichrist, but first you should realize how little the Bible has to say about this topic.

Some Christians trained with the popular endtime view think that the book of Revelation is about the coming antichrist and his activity in the world during the end days. In truth, the word "antichrist" is never mentioned even once in the book of Revelation. This fact can be shocking to Christians who have sat for years under popular endtime teaching, because the antichrist is discussed so much in those circles. Since popular endtime teaching associates the antichrist with the book of Revelation, Christians assume that it actually is the revelation of the antichrist in the end days.

In reality, the book is about the revelation of Jesus Christ. It is about Jesus and His activities of taking over this world.*

As we said earlier, there are only four passages in the Bible where the antichrist is mentioned, and all four of these are in I and II John. We already quoted one passage (I John 4:1-3), but now let's look more carefully at that passage to see exactly what John said about this antichrist.

> Beloved, do not believe every spirit, but test the spirits to see whether they are from God, because many false prophets have gone out into the world. By this you know the Spirit of God: every spirit that confesses that Jesus Christ has come in the flesh is from God; and every spirit that does not confess Jesus is not from God; this is the spirit of the antichrist, of which you have heard that it is coming,

---

* We will not be explaining the victorious view of the book of Revelation, but some of the books recommended in the bibliographies will expand your understanding on this subject.

and now it is already in the world.

(I John 4:1-3)

According to John's words, what is the antichrist? It is *a spirit or that which has a spirit which does not confess that Jesus is from God.* According to John's words, *when* was this antichrist active in the Earth? John said it was *"already in the world,"* that is, it was active in the First Century while John was alive. More specifically, John was attributing the activity of the antichrist to the many false prophets who had gone out into the world during his lifetime.

Now let's examine the other passages which mention the antichrist.

I John 2:18 tells us this:

Children, it is the last hour; and just as you heard that antichrist is coming, even now many antichrists have appeared....

In this verse, John does not give us a description nor a definition of the antichrist, but he does expand our understanding, telling us that there are *many antichrists,* not just one. Further, he tells us that they already *"have appeared,"* that is, in John's lifetime.

I John 2:22 adds to our understanding:

Who is the liar but the one who denies that Jesus is the Christ? This is the antichrist, the one who denies the Father and the Son.

33

Here we have a description. The antichrist is the one who denies that Jesus is the Christ and denies the Father and the Son.

Finally, let's look at the fourth and last passage in which the antichrist is mentioned:

> *For many deceivers have gone out into the world, those who do not acknowledge Jesus Christ as coming in the flesh. This is the deceiver and the antichrist.*
>
> (II John 1:7)

Notice John's description of the antichrist: the deceiver who does not acknowledge that Jesus came in the flesh. Do you see how clearly John is fighting the First-Century heretical teaching of Gnosticism? John was speaking of a deceiver that was active in his lifetime.

That's it. There is no other passage in the Bible which mentions the antichrist.

This can be very disturbing to Christians who have been indoctrinated into popular endtime teaching. When told that the word "antichrist" is mentioned only in four Bible passages and never in the book of Revelation, they typically have a hard time accepting it. It is helpful to challenge such people to look in a Bible Concordance themselves, where they actually can see how few Bible passages mention the antichrist. Even after such an exercise, many will be unable to accept the biblical evidence. In fact, one minister friend was presenting the truths of I and II John to a congregation, and a lady spoke out in protest, demanding, "Don't take my antichrist from me!"

It is sad but it is true. Some Christians have their faith so bound up with popular teachings of the antichrist that they cannot bear to have them challenged. If we are going to examine honestly the only four Bible passages that mention the antichrist, we have to conclude that popular endtime teaching on the antichrist was not developed from the Bible. There are no verses which talk about a person called the antichrist, possessed by Satan, starting a false religious system and taking over the world's economic system. The only four verses in the Bible which mention the antichrist all state or imply the antichrist(s) was (were) alive during the First and Second Century. Furthermore, when we understand the historical struggle which the early Church had against Gnosticism, we realize that those brief comments about the antichrist(s) were in reference to false prophets who promoted that heretical way of thinking.

Of course, Christians today can accept the historical evidence of these antichrists in the First and Second Centuries and still imagine some antichrist coming in the future. However, we have to be honest and say people can imagine anything they want, but it is clearly wrong to say that there is *any biblical evidence* suggesting that there will be some antichrist coming in our future. There is no Bible verse that states or implies that.

From where have popular endtime teachers obtained their understanding of the antichrist? Hundreds of books, movies, and videos have built one idea upon another until a scary, threatening image has been developed in the minds of millions of Christians.

35

Active imaginations have been at work building this myth which is fully believed in some branches of Christianity.*

Challenges to Your Faith

This is a good place to talk about the challenges that sincere Christians must face if they are going to allow their beliefs to be tested by the Word of God.

Most Christians, including those holding to the popular endtime view, will claim that their beliefs are based solely on the teachings of the Bible. But everyone of us—no matter how sincere we may be—bring to the Bible, not an empty mind, but a mind full of presuppositions, beliefs, views of reality, experiences, and even political views, which influence the way we see things, and, therefore, influence our interpretation of Scripture. We look at the Bible through a lens of our culture and our view of reality, and, therefore, we can misinterpret the Bible.

Test yourself: have you ever changed your beliefs about something from one viewpoint to another? Everyone who has been a Christian for very long has to answer in the affirmative. The truth is that <u>we</u> use to believe the popular endtime view. As ministers, we

---

* Some of the popular (mis)understanding of the antichrist is the result of popular endtime teachers assuming that the "man of lawlessness," of whom is spoken in II Thessalonians, is the future antichrist. In reality, no Bible verse associates these two concepts. We will say little about the man of lawlessness, but some of the books recommended in the bibliographies thoroughly discuss this subject.

use to teach that view, but we came to be convinced that we had been wrongly influenced by these factors to re-interpret Jesus' words. So we laid our preconceptions aside, and the result was that we changed to what we believe is a much more objective and biblical viewpoint.

Now we are challenging you to lay aside—to the best of your ability—your presumptions, assumptions, and preconceived beliefs about the endtimes—presumptions which you may have picked up, not from the Bible itself, but from novels, movies, and TV preachers. Attempt to re-read Jesus' prophecy as if you were one of His disciples, there at that time sitting on the Mount of Olives. See it through new eyes.

Through many years of presenting biblical truths to various Christian groups, we have observed how people react and struggle when challenged. Christians say they believe the Bible, but most Christians cannot tell you from where in the Bible their own beliefs originated. In fact, we dare say that most Christians believe what they believe, not because they can prove it with the Bible, but because they believe what they were taught by their favorite pastor, Sunday School teacher, Bible teacher, denomination, or television preacher. Of course, we all need teachers to help us see in the Bible the things which we have missed. God is the One Who gives us teachers. However, we should be concerned when Christians are so loyal to one teacher or denomination that they cannot consider seriously the views of other teachers, who also are trying their best to serve the Lord.

We dare say that most Christians will struggle to

hold to their present beliefs, no matter how compelling the historical and biblical evidence is to the contrary. They will hold to those beliefs not because they can defend them biblically, but because of their own loyalty to a spiritual leader whom they love and admire. For them, to question their own beliefs is to be disloyal to the leaders who taught them. It is easier to not question. It is easier to let things remain as they are. Of course, it can be difficult to change. It is difficult to consider other ways of thinking, because you must entertain the possibility that you have been wrong, that teachers whom you love and admire have been wrong, and that you will not know with what to replace your present beliefs if they crumble.

We want to reassure you that if you are willing to go on studying Matthew 24, you will learn what many of your other brothers and sisters in Christ believe. And you will learn some truths that will give you a victorious view of life and the future.

Matthew 24:14: Gospel Preached to the World

As we return to our verse-by-verse study of Matthew 24, remember that we are examining our Lord's answer to the first question which the disciples asked, "When will these things—Jerusalem and the temple—be destroyed?" In light of this question, we are trying to show you that everything Jesus said would happen in Matthew 24:4-34 actually happened in the First Century during the generation in which the disciples lived.

What about Matthew 24:14?

"This gospel of the kingdom shall be preached in the whole world as a testimony to all the nations, and then the end will come."

If you have been trained under the popular endtime view, you know that this verse often is quoted to encourage Christians to help get the gospel spread around the world so that Jesus Christ can return.

Let us show you another way to understand this Scripture. Jesus said that all of the events of which He spoke would happen in that generation. If we are going to believe the words of Jesus literally, then we must look to see how the promise of this verse could have been fulfilled in the First Century.

Any sincere study of Scripture must apply the foundational principles of Bible study, one of these being that other Bible passages which talk about the same topics are read before drawing any conclusions about what a specific passage means. In this way, we allow the Bible to interpret itself, with less misunderstandings due to our own biases and cultural influences.

For example, for us to understand Matthew 24:14, it will be helpful to find out if there are other Bible passages which talk about the gospel being preached to the whole world. If you do this in your own study, you will discover four passages which address this subject. Amazingly, all four passages reveal to us how the gospel was proclaimed to all nations within the generation of the apostles. Let's look at those four passages.

First examine the words of Paul in Romans 1:8:

> *First, I thank my God through Jesus Christ for you all, because your faith is being proclaimed throughout the whole world.*

Is being proclaimed in Paul's lifetime *throughout the whole world.*

Paul makes this even clearer in Romans 10:18:

> *But I say, surely they have never heard, have they? Indeed they have; "Their voice has gone out into all the earth, and their words to the ends of the world."*

Paul tells us this again in Colossians 1:5-6:

> *...the gospel, which has come to you, just as in all the world also it is constantly bearing fruit and increasing....*

There it is again. The gospel was bearing fruit *in all the world,* in Paul's lifetime.

Finally, let's look at the clearest statement Paul made on this subject:

> *If indeed you continue in the faith firmly established and steadfast, and not moved away from the hope of <u>the gospel</u> that you have heard, which <u>was proclaimed in all</u>*

*creation under heaven and of which I,
Paul, was made a minister....*
(Col. 1:23; underlining added)

Could Paul have stated it any clearer? *The gospel was
proclaimed in all creation under heaven.*

As people read these passages they may wonder if
the words "whole world," "ends of the world," "all the
world," and "all creation under heaven," really mean
the whole world in the way we understand today.
Some may question if these words perhaps meant the
world as far as the disciples knew it or just the Roman Empire.

In these passages there are two different Greek
words which have been translated into the word
"world." Paul used the Greek word *kosmos* in Romans
1:8 and in Colossians 1:6. This word *kosmos* can be
translated as "world" or "earth," but either way, it includes the entire world. The other Greek word for
world is *oikoumene,* which can be translated
"inhabited earth" or "civilized earth." Paul used this
word in Romans 10:18, when he declared that the
Word had gone out "to the ends of the world." Jesus
also used this word, *oikoumene,* in Matthew 24:14.
Hence, we understand that His original declaration
was that the disciples would have time to preach the
gospel of the kingdom to the civilized world.

However we look at it, the gospel was preached to
the whole world within the generation of the first disciples. They did turn the world upside down.

41

Justin Martyr
...from Jerusalem there went out into the world, men, twelve in number, and these illiterate, of no ability in speaking: but by the power of God they proclaimed to every race of men that they were sent by Christ to teach to all the world of God.
(First Apology, XXXIX, in The Ante-Nicene Fathers: Translation of the Fathers Down to A.D. 325)

Eusebius
The teaching of the new covenant was borne to all nations, and at once the Romans besieged Jerusalem and destroyed it and the Temple.
(The Proof of the Gospel, I:VI)

Charles H. Spurgeon
It was before that generation had passed away that Jerusalem was besieged and destroyed. There was a sufficient interval for the full proclamation of the gospel by the apostles and evangelists of the early Christian Church, and for the gathering out of those who recognized the crucified Christ as their true Messiah. Then came the awful end, which the Saviour foresaw and foretold, and the prospect of which wrung from his lips and heart the sorrowful lament that followed his prophecy of the doom awaiting his guilty capital.
(The Gospel of the Kingdom, p. 218)

Matthew 24:15-20: Flee from Judea

Jesus told the disciples that after they successfully preached the gospel, they needed to be ready to flee from Judea, because destruction was about to occur.

"Therefore when you see the abomination of desolation which was spoken of through Daniel the prophet, standing in the holy place (let the reader understand), then those who are in Judea must flee to the mountains. Whoever is on the housetop must not go down to get the things out that are in his house. Whoever is in the field must not turn back to get his cloak. But woe to those who are pregnant and to those who are nursing babies in those days! But pray that your flight will not be in the winter, or on a Sabbath." (Matt. 24:15-20)

Christians trained in the popular endtime view envision this passage being fulfilled in the future, sometime before the end of the world. Typically, they think of the abomination of desolation as the antichrist who will walk into the temple in Jerusalem, set up an idol to worship, and declare that he is God. That event is thought to begin a terrible worldwide tribulation.

To understand this passage from the view of victorious eschatology, we first can note that Jesus is talking about tragic events which will happen not

43

throughout the world, but right there in Jerusalem and the surrounding area of Judea. We know this because He is talking to His disciples and answering their question concerning when Jerusalem and the temple will be destroyed. Jesus said that when the abomination of desolation (which we will define later) stands in the holy place, people "in Judea" are to run to the mountains. He did not say that people all over the world should flee. Further, we know that Jesus was addressing His warning to Jews, for He warned people to pray that their flight may not be on the Sabbath—a warning which only is relevant to Jewish people, as they kept the Sabbath in a fashion which did not allow them to work or run—even in the event of a tragedy. Also, He said people on their housetops must not go into their houses to get their possessions; that, too, indicates that He was talking about people in that region of the world, for houses in Jerusalem typically were constructed in a way in which people could gather on their rooftops. Jesus' warning tells us nothing about people living outside of Judea. Jesus was speaking of something terrible about to happen in Judea, and there is nothing in the passage to indicate a worldwide event.

The Parallel Passages in Luke 21 and Mark 13

To further understand Matthew 24:15-22, it would be helpful to read other Bible passages which use the same terminology and address the same topics. This is especially relevant with this passage because both the Gospels of Luke and Mark record parallel passages in which Jesus sat with His disciples on the Mount of Olives and answered their inquiry concerning the coming destruction of Jerusalem and the temple. Let's examine those passages.

In looking at these parallel passages, it is important that we first note how closely they correspond with Matthew 24.

1. Jesus talked about the wickedness of the Jewish religious leaders (Matt. 23:1-35; Mark 12:38-40; Luke 20:45-47).
2. Jesus declared the temple's destruction (Matt. 23:37-24:2; Mark 13:1-2; Luke 21:5-6).
3. The disciples questioned Jesus about the coming destruction (Matt. 24:3; Mark 13:3-4; Luke 21:7).
4. Jesus answered talking about:
   people claiming to be Christ (Matt. 24:5; Mark 13:5-6; Luke 21:8),
   wars and rumors of war (Matt. 24:6-7; Mark 13:7-8; Luke 21:9-10),
   earthquakes and famines (Matt. 24:7; Mark 13:8; Luke 21:11),
   the gospel being preached over the world (Matt. 24:14; Mark 13:10).

These passages are amazingly similar, although each writer used slightly different terminology.

The slight differences may be the result of the different writers recording what they each remembered or considered most important. The differences also could be the result of different occasions on which Jesus talked about this subject. They often were in the temple in Jerusalem, and Jesus would have had many opportunities to talk about the incredible destruction about to occur. Whatever the reasons for the slight differences, we can see that the answers Jesus gave were very similar in each of the three Gospel accounts.

After Jesus talked about the signs that would take place, He went on in each Gospel to warn that the people will have to flee from Judea. Let's examine the accounts in the three parallel passages.

> *"Therefore when you see the abomination of desolation which was spoken of through Daniel the prophet, standing in the holy place (let the reader understand), then those who are in Judea flee to the mountains."*　　　(Matt. 24:15-16)

> *"But when you see Jerusalem surrounded by armies, then recognize that her desolation is near. Then those who are in Judea must flee to the mountains,...."*
> (Luke 21:20-21)

> *"But when you see the abomination of desolation standing where it should not be (let the reader understand), then those who are in Judea must flee to the mountains."*　　　(Mark 13:14)

As we mentioned earlier, popular endtime teachers assume that the abomination is the antichrist who someday in the future will set up an idol in the temple or actually step into the temple and declare himself as God.

To see how unfounded that understanding is, first note that the antichrist never is mentioned here (nor does Jesus ever mention the antichrist). Also, note that Jesus was talking *to His disciples* and telling *them* that *they* will witness this event. Jesus was not talking about an antichrist which would come hundreds or even thousands of years later, but rather some abomination which would be seen in their lifetimes.

Next, we can identify where the abomination was to stand. Matthew refers to the "holy place" and Luke refers to "Jerusalem." Which author is correct? Both. When Matthew mentions the holy place, he was referring to the same location as Luke when he referred to Jerusalem.

We can confirm this by examining the terminology "holy place," which has been translated from the Greek words *hagios topos*. This terminology never is used anywhere in the Bible to refer to the temple or the holy of holies in the temple. As anyone with a Greek dictionary can learn, the word *topos* refers to a locality. It is used in expressions such as a "desert place" and never in reference to a building.

Since we have Luke referring to this holy place as Jerusalem, it is only natural to conclude that Jesus was referring to Jerusalem in the parallel passage of Matthew.

Next, what is the abomination of desolation? When we speak of an abomination, we are referring to a horrible, detestable, disgusting thing. Luke tells us that the abomination was the *armies surrounding Jerusalem*. What could be more detestable to Jewish people? The heathen armies would gather to make the holy city a desolation.

> **St. John Chrysostom**
> The abomination of desolation means that army by which the holy city of Jerusalem was made desolate. (*The Ante-Nicene Fathers: Translation of the Fathers Down to A.D. 325*)

Does this correspond with historical evidence? Perfectly! As we have noted, in the year 70 AD, 20,000 Roman soldiers lined the mountains around Jerusalem, surrounding the holy city.

This matches the description we read in Daniel, chapter nine. Remember Jesus referred in Matthew 24:15 to the abomination of desolation *"about which Daniel spoke."* We will examine the book of Daniel more later, but here note Daniel's reference to the abomination:

> *"...the people of the prince who is to come will destroy the city and the sanctuary. And its end will come with a flood; even to the end there will be war; desolations are determined."* (Daniel 9:26)

Indeed, the soldiers came to destroy Jerusalem. For four months they starved the people, then they descended upon the city as a flood pouring into a valley. When the abomination, that is the Roman soldiers, began lining the mountains around Jerusalem, there was a short time during which people could flee from the city. Hence, we can understand our Lord's exhortation for those on the housetops not to go down to get their possessions, nor those in the field to return to get their cloaks. Jesus was telling them that they must flee immediately. After those first Jerusalem dwellers were allowed to escape, the Roman soldiers sealed off Jerusalem. No one else was allowed to go in or out. The Romans cut the city off so the people would starve.

Josephus wrote:

> So all hope of escaping was now cut off from the Jews, together with their liberty of going out of the city. Then did the famine widen its progress, and devoured the people by whole houses and families; the upper rooms were full of women and children that were dying by famine; and the lanes of the city were full of the dead bodies of the aged; the children also and the young men wandered about the marketplaces like shadows, all swelled with the famine, and fell down dead, wheresoever their misery seized them.   (v:xii:3)

Historically, we know that the early disciples fled

Jerusalem as soon as the soldiers began surrounding the city. Why did they flee? Because they remembered the warning which Jesus gave them, that the city would be surrounded by armies, and they must flee to escape the destruction to follow.

Eusebius
The whole body, however, of the church at Jerusalem, having been commanded by a divine revelation, entrusted to men of approved piety there before the war, removed from the city, and dwelt at a certain town beyond the Jordan, called Pella.
(*Ecclesiastical History*, III, 5:86)

Charles H. Spurgeon
The Christians in Jerusalem and the surrounding towns and villages, "in Judea" availed themselves of the first opportunity for eluding the Roman armies, and fled to the mountain city of Pella, in Perea, where they were preserved from the general destruction which overthrew the Jews. There was no time to spare before the final investment of the guilty city; the man "on the house-top" could "not come down to take anything out of his house," and the man "in the field" could not "return back, to take his clothes." They must flee to the mountains in the greatest haste the moment that they saw "Jerusalem compassed with armies."
(*Matthew: The Gospel of the Kingdom*, p. 215)

The Venerable Bede

...when on the approach of the war with Rome and the extermination of the Jewish people, all the Christians who were in that province, warned by the prophecy, fled far away, as Church history relates, and retiring beyond Jordan, remained for a time in the city of Pella under the protection of Agrippa. (Cited in: Thomas Aquinas' *Golden Chain*, 1956)

Matthew 24:21-22: A Great Tribulation

Jesus warned the disciples to flee from Jerusalem and Judea (Matt. 24:15-20). Then He prophesied the great destruction to follow:

> *"For then there will be a great tribulation, such as has not occurred since the beginning of the world until now, nor ever will. Unless those day had been cut short, no life would have been saved; but for the sake of the elect those days will be cut short."*

Popular endtime teaching says that this great tribulation will come in our future, just before the end of the world, and it will spread over all the Earth. This coming tribulation is talked about so much in some Christian circles that it has developed its own identity and is called "The Great Tribulation."

In reality, Jesus was talking about the destruction

51

of Jerusalem in 70 AD. He was answering the disciples' question, "When will Jerusalem and the temple be destroyed?"

If Jesus truly was talking about the events of 70 AD, then we have another question to answer. How could He have said that nothing so terrible has occurred since the beginning of the world until now, nor ever will? Haven't there been more wicked things happen than the destruction of Jerusalem? What about the holocaust when six million Jews were murdered? What about other times of war and destruction?

The destruction of Jerusalem was not the greatest *in magnitude*, but Jesus was talking in terms of it being the greatest calamity in the sense of suffering and anguish.

Josephus describes to us what actually took place in 70 AD. After the city was sealed off by the Roman soldiers, Josephus tells how the Jews committed terrible atrocities to each other, even horrific actions, such as cannibalism, which occurred during the famine. He narrates a vile account of a woman murdering her son, cooking him and eating half of him, then arguing with thieves who broke into her house looking for food, as to who would eat the other half.

The Jews also swallowed diamonds and precious stones in hopes of safely carrying them to new locations. Knowing this, the Roman soldiers would capture individuals from the city and cut open their stomachs and entrails, searching for whatever they could find.

After Titus put an end to those searchings, a new

form of torture began. Josephus wrote that as men tried to escape the city or to crawl out to gather food, the Roman soldiers would cut off their hands and send them back inside the city. When the Roman soldiers finally were given the order to descend upon Jerusalem, Josephus tells us, more than 500 men were caught per day, then whipped, tortured, and crucified. Men were nailed to crosses in front of the city until there was no more space. Finally, the soldiers entered the city and every person was killed except for 97,000 who were taken away to be slaves in the Egyptian mines or as gifts to various provinces that they might be killed in the theatres.*

When Jerusalem was destroyed, a genocide of Jews was triggered throughout the surrounding regions. Josephus said:

> There was not any one Syrian city which did not slay their Jewish inhabitants, and were not more bitter enemies to us than were the Romans themselves.
>
> (vii:viii:7)

History provides many similar reports of what took place throughout the whole of the Roman Empire.

When we compare the genocide of 70 AD to the Jewish Holocaust of the Twentieth Century we must admit that the Holocaust was greater in number with six million Jews killed over a six year period. However, most of those people were killed with poisonous gas and as far as we know, no one was crucified. In 70

---

* Flavius Josephus, *The Wars of the Jews,* v:xi:1-2; vi:ix:2-3.

AD over one million Jews were tortured, starved, and killed in a four-month period. Despite the Twentieth Century Holocaust's larger magnitude, the violence during the 70 AD tribulation was far more extreme in atrocities committed.

Eusebius
...thousands and thousands of men of every age who together with women and children perished by the sword, by starvation, and by countless other forms of death...all this anyone who wishes can gather in precise detail from the pages of Josephus's history. I must draw particular attention to his statement that the people who flocked together from all Judaea at the time of the Passover Feast and—to use his own words—were shut up in Jerusalem as if in a prison, totalled nearly three million.
(*The History of the Church,* p. 112)

Charles H. Spurgeon
The destruction of Jerusalem was more terrible than anything that the world has ever witnessed, either before or since. Even Titus seemed to see in his cruel work the hand of an avenging God. Truly, the blood of the martyrs slain in Jerusalem was amply avenged when the whole city became a veritable *Aceldama,* or field of blood.
(*Commentary on Matthew,* p. 412)

Matthew 24:23-27: False Christs Appear

As people were being slaughtered throughout Judea, many Jews held to their hopes of a messiah appearing to deliver them at the last moment. Several leaders took advantage of this belief which was so fundamental to the Jewish heart and mind. Knowing this would happen, Jesus gave a warning:

> *"Then if anyone says to you, 'Behold, here is the Christ,' or 'There He is,' do not believe him. For false Christs and false prophets will arise and will show great signs and wonders, so as to mislead, if possible, even the elect. Behold, I have told you in advance. So if they say to you, 'Behold, He is in the wilderness,' do not go out, or 'Behold, He is in the inner rooms,' do not believe them. For just as the lightning comes from the east and flashes even to the west, so will the coming of the Son of Man be."*
> (Matt. 24:23-27)

Josephus wrote of many false prophets and leaders claiming to be the Christ. One example he gave was of a false prophet who publicly declared to the desperate Jerusalem dwellers that on a certain day God was going to supernaturally deliver them. Many Jews followed that leader and ended up loosing their lives because of the their foolish hope. Josephus also described how extraordinary signs appeared includ-

55

ing a star resembling a sword appearing over Jerusalem and then a great light appearing around the temple for half an hour.*

Jesus told the disciples not to listen to any declarations or rumors of Christs or false prophets appearing. Then He made a declaration contrasting the false to the real. He said:

> *"For just as the lightning comes from the east and flashes even to the west, so will the coming of the Son of Man be."*

From this they were to know that Jesus' coming would not happen in the wilderness or in some secret place. When the Messiah truly came, Jesus said, it would happen up above.

Matthew 24:28: The Corpse and Vultures

> *"Wherever the corpse is, the vultures will gather."*

Envision thousands of soldiers gathered on the mountains encircling Jerusalem. Now add to that picture the banner under which they assembled—the banner of the vulture which Roman soldiers carried on flags and often painted on their shields. As a Prophet, Jesus declared that the vultures would gather and Jerusalem would be the corpse.**

---

* Flavius Josephus, *The Wars of the Jews*, vi:v:3.
** In that region of the world the eagle is considered a vulture.

Confirmation from the Parallel Gospels

Jesus finished answering the first question having explained all of the signs which would lead up to the destruction of Jerusalem and the temple. Before we go on to examine His answer to the second question, it is worth pointing out the confirmation of two other Gospels.

We discussed how closely Luke 21 and Mark 13 parallel Matthew 24. There is, however, one key difference. In Matthew 24:3 the disciples asked Jesus three questions:

Question #1: *"When will these things happen?"*
Question #2: *"What will be the sign of Your coming?"*
Question #3: *"What about the end of the age (world)?"*

In contrast, neither Luke nor Mark record the second or third questions. Luke 21:5-7 goes like this:

> *And while some were talking about the temple, that it was adorned with beautiful stones and votive gifts, He said, "As for these things which you are looking at, the days will come in which there will not be left one stone upon another which will not be torn down." They questioned Him, saying, "Teacher, when therefore will these things happen? And what will be the sign when these things are about to take place?"*

Mark 13:1-4 reads very similar to this passage, without asking anything about the signs of our Lord's coming or of the end of the world.

This is significant because it gives us a clear framework in which to understand Matthew 24. Since Luke and Mark only record the question about when the temple would be destroyed, we know that our Lord was answering that question when He talked about people claiming to be Christ, wars, earthquakes, famines, persecutions, etc. The answers Jesus gave in Luke and Mark are almost identical to the answers Jesus gave in Matthew 24:4-22. Therefore, it is only reasonable to conclude that Jesus was talking about the temple's destruction when He talked about people claiming to be Christ, wars, earthquakes, famines, persecutions, etc. This is confirmation that Matthew 24:4-22 is answering the first question only.

Acknowledging the parallels in the three Gospels shows us again how wrong popular endtime teaching is when it tries to combine all three questions recorded by Matthew, as if they all are asking about the second coming and end of the world. We will look at the answers Jesus gives to the two remaining questions, and, indeed, we will talk about His coming and the end of the world, because those are the second and third questions. However, make no mistake that the first question was about the destruction of Jerusalem and the temple. That happened in 70 AD, within the generation of the disciples, exactly as Jesus prophesied.

Concluding Remarks about the First Question

We cannot emphasize enough how significant of an event it was when Jerusalem and the temple were destroyed. Jerusalem was "the holy city." Mount Moriah, upon which the temple stood, was the site where Abraham was willing to offer his son Isaac (Gen. 22:2). It also was the place where God appeared to David (II Chron. 3:1). It was the site upon which Solomon had built the first temple. It was there that the high priests offered sacrifices for the sins of the people. It was the center of Jewish life, a deeply sacred site. When the temple was destroyed, the Jewish heritage was destroyed. In one sense, they were cut off from God. They lost their identity. Their religious system was abolished.

The writer of Hebrews explained how the Jewish religious system was abolished and replaced with the New Covenant established through Jesus.

When He said, "A new covenant," He has made the first obsolete. But whatever is becoming obsolete and growing old is ready to disappear. (Heb. 8:13)

It is critical that we identify exactly what God made obsolete when Jesus established the New Covenant. Some people believe that God made obsolete the covenant He had with Abraham and His descendants. That is not true, and we know this because the covenant God made with Abraham was an eternal covenant (Gen. 17:7; 13:15). Paul explained that when

God enacts new agreements with people, they never invalidate a covenant previously ratified by God (Gal. 3:15-17). What, then, was nullified when Jesus made the New Covenant? It was the religious system established through Moses. That was the context of Hebrews 7 to 9, where we are told that the old was abolished. Approximately 430 years after Abraham, Moses was used by God to establish a religious system for Abraham's descendants. We must not confuse that religious system with the covenant God made with Abraham and his descendants. The Abrahamic Covenant is still valid, but the religious system of offering animal sacrifices and approaching God through the high priest was made obsolete.

We have a New Covenant with better promises. We have a High Priest Who has made the ultimate and final sacrifice.

The transition from the old to the new stands right in the center of history and the Bible. It is a pivotal point in God's plan through the ages. When the temple in Jerusalem was destroyed, it finalized the end of the old religious system.

Matthew recorded the second question which the disciples asked Jesus as follows:

"What will be the sign of Your coming?"

Popular endtime teaching understands this question to be about the second coming of our Lord. They say that Jesus will return to Earth after all of the signs of Matthew 24:4-22 occur. In other words, at some point in our future, after wars, earthquakes, famines, persecutions, etc., then Jesus will return.

Victorious eschatology offers a very different understanding. We already explained how all of the signs such as wars, earthquakes, famines, etc., were signs preceding the destruction of the temple in 70 AD. Those signs were fulfilled. They are not for our future.

Now, we need to determine what the disciples meant when they asked, "What will be the sign of Your coming?"

When people read that question today, they have a very different mindset than the disciples 2,000 years ago. When the disciples were sitting with Jesus on the Mount of Olives, they were *not* thinking about the second coming of our Lord. In fact, at that time in their lives they were not convinced that Jesus was going to die (Matt. 16:21-23), let alone return to Earth someday. Therefore, they could not have been asking about the second coming.

What, then, were they asking? Look again at the question: "What will be the sign of Your coming?" What is meant by His "coming?"

At that time in history, the Jews were looking for a Messiah. That was their primary hope. They were looking for a Messiah to come and set up a kingdom in which the Jews would have dominance on Earth and reign forever. Knowing this gives us an entirely different outlook on the thinking of the disciples.

Remember when the mother of the sons of Zebedee asked Jesus if her two sons could sit, one on His right and the other on His left (Matt. 20:20-23)? That reveals what was on their minds.

When the disciples asked Jesus, "What will be the sign of Your coming," they were asking Him, "When will You come into Your kingdom?" "When will You take Your position and reveal Yourself as King?"

When did that happen? After Jesus died, resurrected, and ascended into heaven, He sat down on a throne at the right hand of God. All authority was given to Him, both in heaven and Earth. Jesus came into His kingdom the moment He ascended into heaven and sat down next to the Father. It happened almost 2,000 years ago, in the generation in which the disciples lived.

To confirm this, read the words of Jesus in Matthew 16:28:

> *"Truly I say to you, there are some of those who are standing here who will not taste death until they see the Son of Man coming in His kingdom."*

Similarly, Mark records the words of Jesus:

> "...there are some of those who are standing here who will not taste death until they see the kingdom of God after it has come with power." (Mark 9:1)

Could Jesus have said it any clearer? He declared that some of the people who were alive at that time in history would live to see Him come into His kingdom. Indeed, Jesus sat down on His throne 2,000 years ago. With that understanding of "coming into His kingdom," we now can look at our Lord's answer.

As we look at this, do not jump to the conclusion that we reject a belief in the second coming. We know that Jesus will return to Earth at some point in the future, and we will talk about His second coming later when we look at our Lord's answer to the third question. What we are saying at this point is that the disciples' second question was not about Jesus' second coming, but they were inquiring about His coming into His kingdom.

Jesus Answers the Second Question

It is helpful to see how closely associated the destruction of Jerusalem was with the coming of Jesus into His kingdom. Jesus says:

> "But immediately after the tribulation of those days...." (Matt. 24:29)

From this verse on to verse 34, Jesus talks about coming to His kingdom and He answers the disciples' second question.

> **Jonathan Edwards**
> Tis evident that when Christ speaks of his coming, his being revealed, his coming in his Kingdom, or his Kingdom's coming, He has respect to his appearing in those great works of his Power, Justice and Grace, which should be in the Destruction of Jerusalem and other extraordinary Providences which should attend it.
> (*The History of Redemption* 1776, Miscellany #1199)

Matthew 24:30a: The Sign of the Son of Man

> *"And then the sign of the Son of Man will appear in the sky, ..."*

Popular endtime teachers look at these words and envision Jesus appearing in the sky. But look carefully. Does this verse say Jesus will appear in the sky? It says "the sign" will appear. A sign is similar to a billboard declaring something. What is the sign? It is the sign of the Son of Man. It is not Jesus Who will appear, but the sign which will appear.

The *King James Version* of Matthew 24:30 reads like this:

> *"And then shall appear the sign of the*

Son of man in heaven...."

Again, careful reading leads us to see that it is not Jesus Who appears, but the sign that appears. And what will that sign indicate? That the Son of Man is in heaven. He had arrived. He had sat down on His throne. He made it!

Notice that the *King James Version* refers to the Son of Man in "heaven," while the *New American Standard Bible* (which we quoted earlier) refers to the Son of Man in the "sky." Either translation is correct because the Greek word *ourano* may be translated as either "heaven" or "sky." However, if we use the word "sky," the reader may envision Jesus up above in the clouds. On the other hand, if we understand that Jesus is in "heaven," then we may envision Him with His Father sitting on His throne. It is this vision in heaven which corresponds with Jesus' coming into His kingdom.

Put yourself in the shoes of the disciples 2,000 years ago sitting on the Mount of Olives. They soon were going to lose the One Whom they had been following. He would die. After Jesus ascended into heaven, how were they to know that He actually had made it into heaven? How would they know that He had been given all authority over heaven and Earth?

That is precisely what Jesus was telling them. He was answering the question, "What will be the sign of Your coming into Your kingdom?"

And what is that sign?

Jesus had just told them about all the signs that would end in the destruction of Jerusalem and the temple. That destruction was the sign. It was the billboard. Once they saw the destruction of Jerusalem and the temple, they were to know without a doubt that Jesus Christ was on His throne in heaven.

To gain an understanding of the impact that sign had on the First-Century Jewish disciples, compare it with what happened to Japan in 1945 when atomic bombs were dropped on Hiroshima and Nagasaki. When those bombs decimated the two cities, Japanese people who watched from a distance realized that the war was over. They had lost and the United States was in control.

More people died when Jerusalem was destroyed in 70 AD, than when the two atomic bombs were dropped in Japan. The Jewish nation fell. The temple was destroyed. That was the sign.

When the temple was destroyed the Jewish religious system was ended. No longer could people approach God through the temple with animal sacrifices. There was a new High Priest. The Stone which the builders had rejected had become the Chief Cornerstone. There was a new temple being built out of living stones.

That was the sign that Jesus came into His kingdom. The throne of David had been lifted to heaven. From there Jesus Christ would rule over His kingdom forever.

Matthew 24:29: The Signs of Judgment

"But immediately after the tribulation of those days the sun will be darkened, and the moon will not give its light, and the stars will fall from the sky, and powers of the heavens will be shaken."

To understand this passage, first notice the time frame. Jesus said these things would happen *"immediately after the tribulation of those days."* Since the tribulation which Jesus described happened in 70 AD, we must look for the fulfillment *"immediately"* after 70 AD.

To see the fulfilment of this, we need to be familiar with certain Jewish idioms. The sun, the moon, and the stars frequently were used to refer to governing authorities. For example, Joseph had a dream in which the sun, moon, and stars all bowed down to him (Gen. 37:9); when Joseph relayed this dream to his family, they did not conclude that the sun, moon, and stars literally would bow, but they immediately knew the implied meaning that Joseph would be raised above other governing authorities. Similarly, we can read in Revelation 12:1 where a woman appears with the sun and moon under her feet, and with a crown of stars on her head, meaning that she would have great authority.

In biblical terminology, the fame and glory of large cities were said to shine as the sun, moon, or stars. When a certain city was destroyed, the sun, moon, or stars were said to darken.

For example, in the book of Ezekiel we can read about the judgment and coming destruction of Egypt.

> "And when I extinguish you,
> I will cover the heavens and darken their
> stars;
> I will cover the sun with a cloud
> And the moon will not give its light.
> All the shining lights in the heavens
> I will darken over you
> And will set darkness on your land,"
> Declares the Lord God. (Ezek. 32:7-8)

This destruction which was prophesied by Ezekiel happened to Egypt, but there is no record of the sun, moon, and stars literally going dark.

We can understand this when we realize that prophets sometimes spoke in this apocalyptic terminology. We can compare it with some modern-day idioms which people may use when tragedy strikes: "His life caved in around him!" "They pulled the rug out from under him!" "The sky is falling!" or "The lights went out!" It may be difficult for a modern-day Christian to think of Jesus using such terminology, but that is exactly what He did. In fact, that is the only way we find this terminology used anywhere else in the Bible. It was a Jewish idiom in reference to coming destruction and the transfer of authority.

Consider how Isaiah decreed destruction upon a region south of Israel known as Edom:

> And all the host of heaven will wear

away,
And the sky will be rolled up like a scroll;
All their hosts will also wither away
As a leaf withers from the vine,
Or as one withers from the fig tree.
For My sword is satiated in heaven,
Behold it shall descend for judgment
    upon Edom
And upon the people whom I have
    devoted to destruction. (Is. 34:4-5)

At that time in history the sky was not literally "rolled up like a scroll." The hosts of heaven did not literally fall to the ground as leaves from a fig tree. Yet, Edom was destroyed.

Finally, consider God's declaration of judgment through Isaiah upon Babylon.

For the stars of heaven and their
    constellations
Will not flash forth their light;
The sun will be dark when it rises
And the moon will not shed its light.
(Is.13:10)

When Babylon was judged, there was no record of stars and constellations ceasing from shining. The sun was not dark when it came up. The moon did not dim. Yet destruction came.

If we are going to allow the Bible to interpret itself, then we will conclude that Jesus was using apocalyptic language to declare destruction. Just as the prophets Isaiah and Ezekiel spoke judgments against Egypt, Edom, and Babylon, so also Jesus as a Prophet declared destruction upon Jerusalem. The disciples of Jesus would have recognized that phraseology. They knew the Old Testament. Such terminology was part of their cultural expressions.

This fits perfectly with what actually took place after Jesus died, resurrected, and ascended into heaven. Jesus sat down at the right hand of the Father. He was given all authority over heaven and Earth. The evidence on Earth of Jesus ruling in heaven was that the old temple was destroyed. There was a new High Priest sitting in heaven. There was a new ruler, the King of kings and the Lord of lords.

> ...who is at the right hand of God, having gone into heaven, after angels and authorities and powers had been subjected to Him. (I Pet. 3:22)

The heavens were shaken, because Jesus Christ came into His Kingdom.

Matthew 24:30b: The Son of Man in Glory

We already have examined the first part of Matthew 24:30 (p. 64-66), but now let's consider the rest of the verse.

> "And then the sign of the Son of Man will appear in the sky, and then all the tribes of the earth will mourn, and they will see

the Son of Man coming on the clouds of the sky with power and great glory. "

What does it mean, *"then all the tribes of the earth will mourn"*? To answer this, we need to examine the Greek word *ge* which has been translated in this version to "earth." Some other Bible versions translate this word *ge* as "land," which we believe is truer to the context of this passage. Hence, all of the tribes of the land shall mourn. Who are the tribes of the land? The land of which is spoken in this passage is Judea. Therefore, all of the tribes of the Jews will mourn.

When news of the destruction of the temple and of the whole of Jerusalem reached the tribes of Israel, great mourning took place in their synagogues and homes.

The "sign" (the destruction of Jerusalem) caused the "tribes" (of Israel) to mourn greatly, yet they still missed the significance of the sign. It was the sign that "the Son of Man" was "in heaven," that He had ascended back to His Father.

When Jesus referred to *"the Son of Man coming on the clouds of heaven with power and great glory,"* He did not say that the Son was coming back to Earth. This event was to happen in heaven. There Jesus was clothed with power and glory.

This is exactly what Daniel had prophesied as he saw in vision Jesus Christ taking His position at the right hand of the Father:

"I kept looking in the night visions,
And behold, with the clouds of heaven

One like a Son of Man was coming,
And He came up to the Ancient of Days
And was presented before Him.
And to Him was given dominion,
Glory and a kingdom,
That all the peoples, nations and men of
*   every language*
Might serve Him...." (Dan. 7:13-14)

Daniel prophesied it. Then Jesus fulfilled it when He received from His Father the right to rule, His work on Earth being satisfactorily completed.

Matthew 24:31: Angels Gathering the Elect

"And He will send forth His angels with a great trumpet, and they will gather together His elect from the four winds, from one end of sky to the other."

To many people, this only can speak of the second coming of Christ at the end of history. But that is not what Jesus said it meant. Only three verses after this, He states that *"this generation will not pass away until all these things take place."* Jesus said that this verse was descriptive of one of the things which would happen within the span of one generation.

How can we understand this? As Jesus sat down on His throne, all authority was given to Him in heaven and Earth. Everything changed the moment Jesus came into His kingdom. The blowing of a trumpet meant to the Jews that a royal decree was going out. And what was that decree? It was time to release the angels of God to go and gather His people from every nation. At the same time the disciples of Jesus were commanded to go and preach the gospel, making disciples of every nation. No longer was the Jewish nation the only people allowed within a covenant relationship with God. Jesus had become the Good Shepherd Who was gathering His sheep from across the world.

The word "gather" is significant, for it literally means "to synagogue." Christ's messengers would be gathering people together into His New Synagogue. The end of the old temple would only help to hasten the building of the New Temple, which is the Church. It is a simple fact of history that the Church began its vigorous growth after Jerusalem fell.

Matthew 24:32-33: Know that He is Near

"Now learn the parable from the fig tree: when its branch has already become tender and puts forth its leaves, you know that summer is near. So, you too, when you see all these things, recognize that He is near, right at the door."

Jesus is telling the disciples here that just as the budding of a fig tree is a sure sign that summer is near, so also these warning signs were signalling the beginning of a new spiritual season, with the end of the old age and the flourishing of a new one. This lesson of the fig tree is even more powerful if we realize that Jesus and the disciples were sitting on the Mount of Olives. Our Lord easily could have taken a tender branch from a nearby fig tree and given them the lesson to watch for the obvious signs which would indicate the destruction of Jerusalem and then His coming into His kingdom.

Some teachers of the popular endtime view claim that the fig tree is a symbol of Israel and what Jesus is saying is that when Israel is reborn as a nation, the generation which sees it happen also will see the second coming of Christ.

This is an astounding interpretation. In the Bible, Israel typically is pictured as an olive tree, rather than a fig tree (i.e., Jer. 11:16; Rom. 11:17). Furthermore, there is no mention of a rebirth of Israel in this context. Jesus already listed all of the signs for which they were to watch and none of them implies anything about Israel being reborn. In the context, Jesus was not talking about an event 2,000 years in the future. Jesus was answering His disciples' questions about His coming into His kingdom—an event which they would see in their lifetimes.

We can know that the fig tree illustration was not about the future rebirth of Israel and the second coming of Jesus because the next verse is the Lord's declaration that all of the signs would happen in that generation (24:34). Furthermore, that would contradict what Jesus says two verses later (24:36) about there being *no signs* to indicate when His *second* coming would occur (a subject we will discuss shortly). Jesus would not talk about looking at the obvious signs and then immediately say that He does not even know the day and the hour of His return.

For anyone who needs more proof, we also can know that the fig tree illustration was not about the rebirth of Israel and that generation seeing the second coming of Jesus because it is not true! Israel became a nation in 1948, and more than 50 years have passed without Jesus' return.

The obvious, simple lesson of the fig tree was to watch for all the signs listed in Matthew 24:4-28. When those signs were fulfilled, the disciples were to know that Jesus had come into His kingdom.

Matthew 24:34: In this Generation

Jesus ended His answer to the disciples' second question by saying:

> *"Truly I say to you, this generation will not pass away until all these things take place."*

If we take these verses literally as written, then we will believe that everything Jesus prophesied in Matthew 24:5-34 was fulfilled by 70 AD.

Of course, popular endtime teachers cannot accept the words of Jesus literally. Sometimes they redefine the word "generation" (*genesis*, in Greek) to be "race," and hence, they can claim that all of the events listed in Matthew 24 will happen before the race of the Jews passes away.

In reality, that reinterpretation is inconsistent with the rest of the New Testament. The Greek word *genesis* is used 34 times in the New Testament, and never is it translated as "race" in any commonly used translation of the Bible.

If we simply accept the natural and literal meaning of Jesus' statement, we will conclude that all of the events recorded, including the coming of the Lord, happened within the lifetime of the disciples who were listening to Jesus at that time.

John Calvin

Christ informs them, that before a single *generation* shall have been completed, they will learn by experience the truth of what he has said. For within fifty years the city was destroyed and the temple was razed, the whole country was reduced to a hideous desert....

(*Commentary on the Harmony of the Evangelists, Matthew, Mark, and Luke*, vol. 3, p. 151)

The third question the disciples asked pertains to the end of the age (Matt. 24:3). As we mentioned earlier, the Greek word for age, *aion,* is translated in some Bible versions as "world," and, therefore, it may be understood that the disciples were asking about the end of the world. In the following discussion we will use the term "age," but the end of the age definitely will be the end of the world as we know it.

Jesus Answers the Third Question

Jesus answered the third question of the disciples in Matthew 24:35-25:46. Christians who have a red-letter edition of the Bible (that is an edition where all the words of Jesus are printed in red) will notice that Matthew 24:35-25:40 are all the words of Jesus. It is one long discourse in which Jesus answers the question about the end of the age.

We will go through these verses passage by passage, but first it is important to identify how we know Matthew 24:35 is where Jesus begins answering the third question. We did not arbitrarily choose this as the verse in which He began, but a quick examination of the Scriptures reveals that this is, indeed, where Jesus started talking about the end of the age. Allow us to explain.

We already studied Matthew 24:34, where Jesus

said everything preceding that verse would happen in that generation. He was giving a notable break and a reasonable place for us to see how the events after Matthew 24:34 could happen at a later date, in a later generation.

Further, we can note the next verse where Jesus begins answering the third question:

> *"Heaven and earth will pass away, but My words will not pass away."*

Jesus is emphasizing how His words certainly will come true, but He also is making a statement about the end of things—heaven and Earth passing away. That is what the disciples asked in their third question: *"What about the end of the age (world)?"*

Finally, we can know that this is where Jesus began answering the third question because He starts talking about "the day and hour":

> *"But of that day and hour no one knows, not even the angels of heaven, nor the Son, but the Father alone."* (Matt. 24:36)

When the Bible uses the terminology, "the day and hour," or "the Great Day," or "the Last Day," or in some contexts "the Day," it refers to judgment day, and not just any judgment day, but the Final Great Judgment Day when God will call all people to account at the end of the world (see Matt. 7:22; Luke 10:12; John 6:39; 12:48; Rom. 2:16; I Cor. 1:8; 3:13; 5:5; Phil. 1:6; 1:10; II Thes. 1:10; II Tim. 1:18; 4:8;

Heb. 10:25; II Peter 3:10, 12; Jude 1:6).

That Final Great Judgment Day is the topic of the rest of Matthew 24 and all of Matthew 25. Jesus compares the Great Judgment Day with the Judgment of Noah's Flood (24:37-39), two men in a field (24:40-41), a thief coming in the night (24:42-44), a master returning to demand his servants give an accounting (24:45-51), a groom returning for his bride (25:1-13), and a master returning to see how his servants have used their talents (25:14-30). Jesus ends this great teaching by talking about the Son of Man coming in glory with all of the angels, and then the nations being gathered before Him (Matt. 25:31-46).

We briefly will examine each of these passages, but notice that each talks about the coming judgment and the returning Judge. Hence, we understand that Jesus is answering the third question concerning the end of the age (or world).

Charles H. Spurgeon
There is a manifest change in our Lord's words here, which clearly indicate that they refer to His last great coming to judgment.
(*The Gospel of the Kingdom*, p. 218)

Matthew 24:36: No One Knows When

> *"But of that day and hour no one knows,*
> *not even the angels of heaven, nor the*
> *Son, but the Father alone."*

The key point of this passage is that the day of the Lord will be a surprise. Jesus did not know when it would come. The angels did not know. Only the Father knew. Jesus went on to explain that it will come with no warning.

Notice how different our Lord's answer to this question is than to the other two questions. Concerning the destruction of Jerusalem, Jesus said there would be time to preach the gospel and then armies would surround Jerusalem. Concerning our Lord's coming into His kingdom, Jesus said the primary visible sign would be the destruction of Jerusalem and the temple. However, concerning the end of the age, Jesus said, *"no one knows, not even the angels of heaven, nor the Son."*

This surprise element of the end of the age is a fundamental theme of each of the parables which Jesus gave in the rest of Matthew 24 and all of Matthew 25.

Matthew 24:37-39: As the Days of Noah

"For the coming of the Son of Man will be just like the days of Noah. For as in those days before the flood they were eating and drinking, marrying and giving in marriage, until the day that Noah entered the ark, and they did not understand until the flood came and took them all away; so will the coming of the Son of Man be."

Jesus wanted to impress upon the disciples' minds (and our minds) that the final day of judgment will come as a surprise. Just as in Noah's day, people will be eating and drinking, marrying and giving in marriage, then suddenly, Jesus will appear and Judgment Day will have arrived.

Matthew 24:40-42: As Two Men in the Field

"Then there will be two men in the field; one will be taken and one will be left. Two women will be grinding at the mill; one will be taken and one will be left. Therefore be on the alert, for you do not know which day your Lord is coming."

The primary point of this passage is that the Great Judgment Day will come suddenly, and therefore, people should always be alert.

Matthew 24:43-44: As a Thief in the Night

Next, Jesus taught the surprise element with a parable of a thief coming in the night.

"But be sure of this, that if the head of the house had known at what time of the night the thief was coming, he would not have allowed his house to be broken into. For this reason you also must be ready; for the Son of Man is coming at an hour

when you do not think He will."

Not only will the Great Judgment Day arrive without warning, but it will come when you do not expect it. Therefore, be ready at all times.

Matthew 24:45-51: As a Master Returning

"Who then is the faithful and sensible slave whom his master put in charge of his household to give them their food at the proper time? Blessed is that slave whom his master finds so doing when he comes. Truly I say to you that he will put him in charge of all his possessions. But if that evil slave says in his heart, 'My master is not coming for a long time,' and begins to beat his fellow slaves and eat and drink with drunkards; the master of that slave will come on a day when he does not expect him and at an hour which he does not know, and will cut him in pieces and assign him a place with the hypocrites; in that place there will be weeping and gnashing of teeth."

There are many lessons that can be taken from this passage, but the most fundamental truth is that Judgment Day will arrive as a surprise with no warning, therefore, the listener is exhorted to continue being diligent in service and living righteously.

Matthew 25:1-13: As Ten Virgins Waiting

In the next passage, Jesus told a parable of ten virgins who were waiting for their groom to come and take them. Five of the virgins were foolish, not ready for the return of the groom, while the other five were wise, staying prepared for the groom.

The most obvious lesson, again, is that God's people must be ready because Jesus could return at any time, without warning.

Matthew 25:14-30: As Servants with Talents

Jesus then offered a parable about a man entrusting his possessions to three servants. To one he gave five talents, to another two, and to the last servant one talent. When the master returned, he demanded that each servant give an account for how he had used the talents. Then he rewarded them each accordingly.

The primary lesson of coming judgment is so obvious, that we do not need to comment.

A secondary lesson is that there would be a great delay before the return of Christ. We see that delay in verse 19 which says:

> "Now *after a long time* the master of those slaves came..." (underlining added)

This delay is unlike the judgment upon Jerusalem which was to happen in that generation.

Matthew 25:31-46: The Great Day of Judgment

In the final passage of Matthew 25, Jesus gave a description and summary of the coming Great Day of Judgment.

> *"But when the Son of Man comes in His glory, and all the angels with Him, then He will sit on His glorious throne. All the nations will be gathered before Him; and He will separate them from one another, as the shepherd separates the sheep from the goats; and He will put the sheep on His right, and the goats on the left. Then the King will say to those on His right, 'Come, you who are blessed of My Father, inherit the kingdom....' Then He will also say to those on His left, 'Depart from Me, accursed ones, into the eternal fire....' These will go away into eternal punishment, but the righteous into eternal life."*

Again, the lesson is clear: Jesus will return to judge the righteous and the unrighteous.

The third question which the disciples asked, "What about the end of the age?" Jesus clearly had answered.

Summary

The understanding of Matthew 24 and 25, which we have just presented to you, is held by a significant part of the Body of Christ around the world. The reason we mention this is to make clear that we have not presented some bizarre doctrine which no one else believes. Thousands of Christians would explain Matthew 24 very similarly to the way we have just explained it, although they may have slight variations in how they explain individual verses. The view which we presented has even been assigned a theological label by those who study eschatology. It is known as the Partial Preterist View. This is in contrast to two other well-known views, called the Preterist View and the Futurist View.

The Futurist View is what we have been calling today's popular endtime view. Bible teachers call it the Futurist View because it sees all of the events prophesied in Matthew 24:4-51 as taking place in the future, before the end of the world. The Preterist View, which recently has been becoming more accepted in some Christian circles, teaches that all of the events of Matthew 24:4-51 happened during the First Century, by 70 AD.

The view we have come to believe is the Partial Preterist View, which says that the first part of Matthew 24 (vs. 4-34) was fulfilled in the First Century, during the generation in which Jesus spoke those words. The last part of Matthew 24 (vs. 35-51), along with Matthew 25, will be fulfilled in the future at the end of the age.

If you come to believe the view we have just presented, then you will embrace two truths which are dramatically contrary to the popular endtime view:

1. The great tribulation spoken of by Jesus is now long past and will not be in our future.

2. There will be *no signs* preceding the second coming of Jesus or the end of the world.

Concerning tribulation, it is our understanding that difficult times will continue until Jesus Christ has taken full dominion of the world. However, there is no biblical basis to believe in a future period during which the antichrist will rule the world.

Concerning the signs preceding the second coming and the end of the world, they will not be evident to anyone. Jesus did not know of any signs and no one else will be able to figure it out either. Jesus was emphatic about this point, giving no less than six different parables to make sure His followers would understand that it will be a surprise!

This is contradictory to what is spoken of by popular endtime teachers who love to create in their listeners anticipation of the second coming by talking about increasing wars, famines, earthquakes, false religious leaders, and people falling away from the faith. In reality, all of those signs preceded the destruction of Jerusalem in 70 AD. When Jesus returns, at some point in the future, you will be eating and drinking, driving your car, sleeping in bed, or working at your job, when suddenly Jesus Christ will appear in the sky. No warning, no signs.

II. Prophetic Messages
Given to Daniel

Living several hundred years before Jesus came into the world, Daniel recorded visions, dreams, and prophecies concerning the coming of the Messiah, the endtimes, the future of the Jews, and the coming of the Kingdom of God. Here we will examine the divine messages recorded, first in Daniel chapter two, and then in Daniel chapter nine.

The Message of Daniel Chapter Two

Nebuchadnezzar, the king of Babylon, had a dream in which God revealed the future. Daniel was able to tell the king his dream and give its interpretation.

Daniel told King Nebuchadnezzar that he saw in his dream a tremendous statue with a head of fine gold, breast and arms of silver, its belly and thighs of bronze, its legs of iron, and its feet partly of iron and partly of clay. Daniel then told the king that in his dream a rock appeared and that rock crushed the feet of the statue. Then the whole statue was crushed and blown away as dust in the wind. Finally, the stone became a great mountain and filled the whole Earth (Dan. 2:31-35).

Daniel then revealed to the king what the dream meant.

> *"You, O king,...are the head of gold. After you there will arise another kingdom inferior to you, then another third kingdom of bronze,....Then there will be a fourth kingdom as strong as iron...."*
>
> (Dan. 2:37-40)

Daniel told the king that the four parts of the statue represented four kingdoms, one following after the other. Daniel also told King Nebuchadnezzar that his kingdom, the Babylonian kingdom, was the first kingdom. Other passages in the book of Daniel talk

89

further about these four kingdoms and name the Medio-Persian kingdom as the second kingdom (5:28; 8:20), and the Greek Empire as the third kingdom (8:21). Indeed, we know from history that there were four consecutive kingdoms in that region of the world: the Babylonian Empire, the Medio-Persian Empire, the Greek Empire, and the Roman Empire.

**Timeline Showing
The Revelation of Daniel Two:**

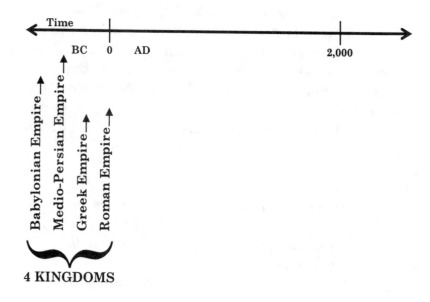

Whether readers believe the popular endtime view or victorious eschatology, they will agree that God was revealing to Daniel that there would be these four earthly kingdoms.

Daniel then explained the rock in Nebuchadnez-zar's dream which crushed those kingdoms and grew into a mountain which filled the Earth.

"In the days of those kings the God of heaven will set up a kingdom which will never be destroyed, and that kingdom will not be left for another people; it will crush and put an end to all these kingdoms, but it will itself endure forever."
(Dan. 2:44)

Daniel revealed that the Rock will come into the Earth, crush all other kingdoms, and bring in the kingdom of God. Then God's kingdom would grow as a mountain which fills the Earth.

Whether readers believe the popular endtime view or victorious eschatology, they will agree that the Rock is Jesus Christ coming into the world to establish God's eternal kingdom and that kingdom would replace all other kingdoms.

The two different views *disagree* concerning the *timing* of when the Rock comes into the Earth and when the kingdom of God gets established. Allow us to explain.

Popular Endtime Understanding of Daniel Two

The popular endtime view teaches that God's kingdom will be brought into the Earth after a seven-year tribulation, at the second coming of Jesus Christ.

Then the kingdom of God will be upon the Earth for 1,000 years.

Timeline of Daniel Two
According to the Popular Endtime View:

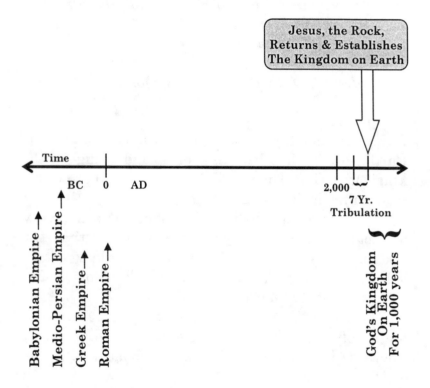

Victorious View of Daniel Chapter Two

Those who hold to victorious eschatology believe that God's kingdom was established almost 2,000 years ago when Jesus came the first time. Jesus came declaring that the kingdom of God was at hand, meaning it was available and within reach. Jesus established His position as King over that kingdom when He ascended into heaven and sat down at the right hand of God. Since that day the kingdom gradually has been growing to maturity, and eventually it will fill the whole Earth, as the mountain in Nebuchadnezzar's dream.

Timeline of Daniel Two
According to Victorious Eschatology:

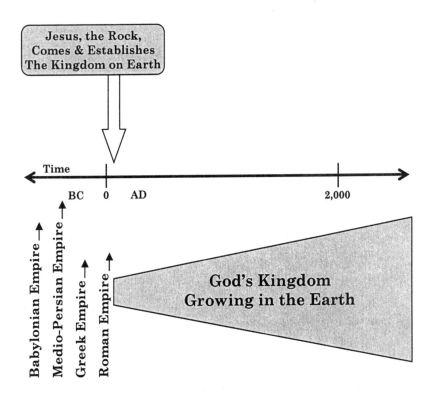

Victorious eschatology teaches that the kingdom of God eventually will fill the Earth, however, evil will remain in the Earth until the second coming of Jesus. We can see this by examining our Lord's parable concerning the man who sowed seeds in his field. Those seeds grew to maturity, but an enemy sowed tares in the same field and those tares also grew. As Jesus explained this parable to His disciples, it is clear that both good and evil are growing in the Earth. Both the good and the evil will be allowed to grow together until the day Jesus returns and separates one from the other (Matt. 13:24-43).

In another parable, Jesus compared the kingdom with a mustard seed growing into the biggest tree in a garden. In similar fashion, the kingdom of God has been growing in the Earth and one day will be the biggest, most influential entity on the Earth, even though there shall be other plants which are not of God's kingdom (Matt. 13:31-32).

This is exactly what we see happening historically since Jesus sat down on His throne. Christianity started off in one small region in the Middle East with one Leader and twelve followers. Today, 2,000 years later, it is the largest religion covering the face of the Earth. Out of six billion people, over two billion claim to be Christians today.

The Roman Empire

Daniel's interpretation of the king's dream reveals that the Rock comes into the Earth at the time of the fourth kingdom, which is the Roman Empire.

Since the popular endtime view teaches that God's kingdom will come into the Earth at the second coming of Jesus, they must identify some Roman Empire which will be in a ruling position at the time Jesus returns. Some popular endtime teachers say that there must be a "Revived Roman Empire" in the Earth at that time. Some teachers are looking at the United Nations or the European Union as this Revived Roman Empire. Others say that the Roman Catholic Church is the Roman Empire which the Rock soon will come and crush.

Since popular endtime teachers envision the antichrist playing a central role in the endtimes, they typically place that evil ruler as head or in a place of great influence in the Roman kingdom which will be destroyed by the Rock. That belief leaves them very critical and suspicious of the Roman Catholic Church or any Roman governmental entity which they think may be in power at the time of our Lord's return.

Victorious eschatology is not looking for a Revived Roman Empire. Adherents believe the Rock came into the Earth 2,000 years ago. Jesus came and established the kingdom of God during the First Century when the Roman Empire actually was in power.

Summary

If you embrace the victorious understanding of Daniel chapter two, you will believe that the kingdom of God was established when Jesus came to Earth 2,000 years ago. You will not be looking for a Revived Roman Empire. You will not be suspiciously watching various governments associated with that area of the world where Rome once ruled, nor will you be suspicious of the Roman Catholic Church becoming that Roman Empire. The Rock which came into the Earth caused the Roman Empire to crumble, exactly as the words of Daniel revealed.

If you embrace the victorious view, you will realize that it is possible to experience and walk in the kingdom today. That kingdom consists of *"righteousness and peace and joy in the Holy Spirit"* (Rom. 14:17). As you seek first God's kingdom you will experience the blessings of God through which *"all these things* [food, clothing, and other provisions] *are added unto you"* (Matt. 6:33).

Many Christians who believe the popular endtime view will try to claim these benefits, but then a moment later they will teach that the kingdom of God will not be available until the second coming of Jesus.

If you embrace the victorious view, you will be confidently looking for God's kingdom to grow—advancing everyday. When Jesus Christ returns, He will subdue all evil, and establish His perfect will throughout the world. Since God's kingdom is advancing progressively in the Earth, you can confidently say that God's kingdom is here and it is growing.*

---

* For more teaching about the advancing kingdom of God, see Harold R. Eberle's book entitled, *Bringing the Future into Focus*.

The Message of Daniel Chapter Nine

In Daniel chapter nine, we read about Daniel praying for his people, the Jews. At that time in history, the Jews were in captivity in Babylon. Their holy city, Jerusalem, was standing in ruins. Daniel knew that God would free His people from their bondage, for it had been promised through earlier prophets (Dan. 9:2). Daniel confessed the sins of his people and asked for mercy (9:3-19). Then God sent the angel Gabriel to Daniel, and Gabriel told Daniel what would be the future of the Jews and Jerusalem.

The words which Gabriel declared reveal not only the future of the Jews and Jerusalem, but also some significant facts about our future and the future of the world. However, Gabriel's words are understood differently by those who hold to the popular endtime view than those believing victorious eschatology.

Seventy Weeks for the Jews and Jerusalem

Gabriel's declaration about the future began as follows:

> *"Seventy weeks have been decreed for your people and your holy city, to finish the transgression, to make an end of sin, to make atonement for iniquity, to bring in everlasting righteousness, to seal up vision and prophecy and to anoint the*

most holy place." (Dan. 9:24)

Whether Christians hold to the popular endtime view or to victorious eschatology, they will agree about the meaning of this verse: God had decreed that the Jews and their holy city, Jerusalem, were to experience 70 weeks of God's favor, during which time God would fulfill the prophecies and promises which He previously had made to them.

Both popular endtime teaching and victorious eschatology hold that God's promise of "seventy weeks" equals 490 years. This understanding is because there are seven days in a week, and 70 times 7 equals 490. Study of the prophetic language of that time period leads us to understand these as years, hence, the Jews were promised 490 years of God's favor. Indeed, as we apply this period of time to the actual historical facts, it reveals some remarkable—obviously divine— predictions which are worth our attention.

As Gabriel went on speaking to Daniel, he divided the 490 years into two periods. First he talked about 69 weeks (69 times 7, or 483 years), and then he talked about the last week (7 years). Together these periods total 490 years.

The First Sixty-nine Weeks

Consider Gabriel's decree concerning the first 69 weeks.

"So you are to know and discern that from the issuing of a decree to restore

and rebuild Jerusalem until Messiah the Prince there will be seven weeks and sixty-two weeks [69 weeks or 483 years]; it will be built again, with plaza and moat, even in times of distress."
(Dan. 9:25)

Gabriel gave a precise time for the coming of Messiah. He said that from the decree to rebuild Jerusalem until Messiah there would be seven weeks and sixty-two weeks, that is 483 years.

In the year 457 BC, Artaxerxes, the king of Persia, decreed that the Jews were free to return to their homeland and rebuild Jerusalem and the temple (Ezra 7:12-26). Students of the Old Testament know that the book of Ezra records this historic event when the Jews went back to Jerusalem to rebuild the temple. The book of Nehemiah records when the Jews rebuilt the walls around Jerusalem. Bible scholars and historians generally agree that the decree to rebuild Jerusalem was issued by King Artaxerxes in 457 BC. If we add 483 years to that date, we come to the year 27 AD.

Historians also tell us that Jesus was born in 4 BC, which means He was 30 years old in 27 AD. That was the year in which Jesus was water baptized and a voice came out of heaven saying, *"This is My beloved Son, in whom I am well-pleased"* (Matt. 3:17). After a period of fasting in the wilderness, Jesus revealed Himself as the Messiah and began His public ministry.

Indeed, there were 483 years between the decree

to rebuild Jerusalem and the revealing of Messiah. Gabriel's prophecy was remarkably accurate, and must have been inspired by God, seeing as how it was given several hundred years before Jesus came into to the world.

Timeline Showing the 483 Years Between the Decree and Messiah:

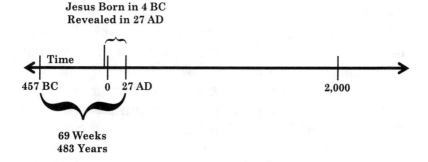

Gabriel went on to declare what would happen after the Messiah came.

> *"Then after the sixty-two weeks the Messiah will be cut off and have nothing, and the people of the prince who is to come will destroy the city and the sanctuary. And its end will come like a flood; even to the end there will be war; desolations are determined."* (Dan. 9:26)

As this verse tells us, Jesus was "cut off." He was put to death.

Then Gabriel said that the people of the prince (the Romans) would come and destroy the city and the sanctuary. Notice how similar Gabriel's wording is to the wording which Jesus used in Matthew 24 and Luke 21: desolations, the end, and destruction as a flood. As we explained earlier, Jerusalem and the temple were destroyed in 70 AD.

Daniel's Seventieth Week

Generally speaking, both the popular endtime view and the view of victorious eschatology agree on how to understand the first 69 weeks (483 years) of God's favor. It is the remaining one week (7 years) about which they disagree. They have different ways of understanding what has become known as "Daniel's Seventieth Week."

Those who hold to the popular endtime view believe that God has not yet given the Jews their last seven years of fulfilling His promises, and, therefore, they conclude that Daniel's seventieth week will have to come in the future. Victorious eschatology, on the other hand, teaches that Daniel's seventieth week already has occurred, and, therefore, we are not still waiting for it to be fulfilled. Allow us to further explain these different understandings.

The Popular View of Daniel's Seventieth Week

Popular endtime teachers will say that before the end of the world, God will turn His favor to the Jews and allow them to return to the Promised Land. Then they will be given seven years of favor, during which time God will fulfill His remaining promises to them, including elevating them as a nation to great authority in the world. During that time the Jews will rebuild the temple in Jerusalem and restore their ancient religious system of offering sacrifices.

With that picture of the Jewish nation arising, popular endtime teachers insert the last verse of Daniel chapter nine.

"And he will make a firm covenant with the many for one week, but in the middle of the week he will put a stop to sacrifice and grain offering...." (Dan. 9:27)

Popular endtime teachers understand that the "he" mentioned in this verse is the antichrist, who, at some point in the future, will make a covenant with the Jews, promising them peace and safety. That covenant will mark the beginning of Daniel's seventieth week. But in the middle of that seven-year period, that is, three-and-a-half years into it, the antichrist will break his covenant, turn against the Jews, and put an end to their religious practice of offering sacrifices to God. Popular endtime teachers understand that God then will begin pouring out His wrath upon the Earth, destroying much of it, but most of all destroying the antichrist and all who follow him.

Popular endtime teaching sees a huge gap— approximately 2,000 years—between the 69 weeks of God's favor and the seventieth week of God's favor upon the Jews. Teachers will explain that in between those two periods God has been focusing on and dealing with the Gentiles, but at some point in the future, He will turn His attention back to the Jews and fulfill His promises to them.

Timeline Showing the Popular Endtime View Of Daniel's Sevenieth Week:

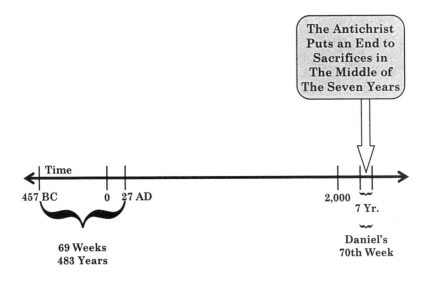

Victorious View of Daniel's Seventieth Week

Victorious eschatology offers a very different understanding of Daniel's seventieth week. Instead of seeing 2,000 years between the 69 weeks and the seventieth week, they see *no gap*. Teachers will explain that in Daniel 9, there is *no gap stated nor implied*. The natural reading of Daniel 9 leads us to believe that the seventieth week follows immediately after the sixty-ninth week.

This understanding has been the understanding of the historic Church. Our forefathers saw no gap between the 69 weeks and Daniel's seventieth week.

Augustine
For let us not suppose that the computation of Daniel's weeks was interfered with...or that they were not complete, but had to be completed afterward in the end of all things, for Luke most plainly testifies that the prophecy of Daniel was accomplished at the time when Jerusalem was overthrown.
(Epistle of Augustine, 199:31, Cited in: Thomas Aquinas' *Golden Chain,* 1956)

If the last seven years of God's favor upon the Jews began immediately after the 69 weeks, then it began in 27 AD, the year Jesus was water baptized and began His public ministry.

If we say that the year 27 AD is the beginning of Daniel's seventieth week, then we must explain how God fulfilled the words of Gabriel when he said, *"in the middle of the week, he will put a stop to sacrifice and grain offering."* Teachers holding to victorious eschatology will say that the "he" spoken of in this verse is Jesus Christ, not the antichrist. In the preceding two verses (Dan. 9:25-26), the Messiah was the main subject, and therefore, it is reasonable to think that in the next verse "he" refers to the Messiah as well.

To see the fulfillment of this, note that three-and-one-half years after Jesus began His public ministry was the Passover when Jesus gave His own life on a cross. On Passover, Jesus shared the Last Supper with His disciples, during which time He took bread and said, *"This is My body..."* and then He took the cup and said, *"This cup is the new covenant in My blood..."* (I Cor. 11:24-25). After sharing that meal, Jesus fulfilled His words by dying on the cross. At that time, *He put an end to sacrifice and offerings.* As the writer of Hebrews explained, Jesus made obsolete the Jewish religious system. A New Covenant had been established and the old system had been abolished. Once the ultimate sacrifice had been made, there no longer was any need for further sacrifices (Heb. 8-9).

Notice how different this understanding is from the popular endtime view. They are looking for the *antichrist* to put an end to the Jewish sacrifices some day in our future. Victorious eschatology believes that *Jesus* put an end to those sacrifices approximately 2,000 years ago.

Eusebius

Now the whole period of our Saviour's teaching and working of miracles is said to have been three and a half years, which is half a week. John the evangelist, in his Gospel makes this clear to the attentive.

(The Proof of the Gospel, bk. 8, chapter 2.)

That explains the first three-and-one-half years of

Daniel's seventieth week, but what about the last three-and-one-half years? The Jews were supposed to experience God's favor and the fulfillment of His promises for a seven-year period. Indeed, they had the Messiah in their midst for the first-three-and-one half years, but what about the three-and-one-half years following the death of Jesus?

If we add three-and-one-half years to the time when Jesus was crucified, we come to another historic event. It was the year in which Stephen was stoned (Acts 7:59-60). Shortly thereafter, Jesus revealed Himself in a blinding light to Saul (Acts 9:1-6). Jesus renamed Saul as Paul, and then He told Paul to go and preach to the Gentiles (Acts 26:15-18). Shortly after that appearance, God spoke to Peter and gave him a vision in which all types of animals were presented to him; then a voice said to Peter, *"Get up, Peter, kill and eat!"* (Acts 10:13). At first Peter refused because he was faithful to the Jewish laws of not eating unclean animals. After meditating on the vision and witnessing a Gentile group receive God's favor, Peter realized that God was declaring that no longer was any person, including Gentiles, to be considered unclean (Acts 10:28).

We cannot emphasize enough how radical a transition this was. The Jews thought of themselves as God's chosen people, separate from the rest of humanity. When God declared the Gentiles as clean, it shook the foundations of Peter's belief system. When Peter went to tell the other Jewish Christians about this, they were indignant that Peter even had associated with Gentiles. Peter had to explain what happened before the other leaders would accept the idea that Gentiles could be saved (Acts 10:1-18).

In the beginning of the book of Acts, the disciples only presented the truths of Jesus Christ to the Jews, for as Paul said to the Jews, *"It was necessary that the word of God be spoken to you first"* (Acts 13:46). However, after three-and-one-half years, God spoke to both Paul and Peter that now they were to present the gospel to all the world.

Timeline Showing
The Victorious View of Daniel's 70th Week:

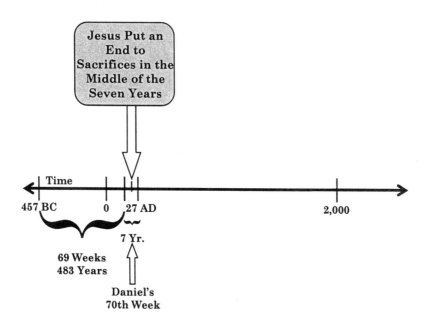

It is with this understanding that we see Daniel's seventieth week fulfilled. Beginning the day Jesus revealed Himself as the Messiah in 27 AD, the Jews were given seven years of favor: three-and-one-half years during which Jesus walked among them, and then another three-and-one-half years during which the disciples preached the good news to the Jews. The Jews received God's greatest favor ever extended to humanity in that they were the first to be exposed to the Messiah, the Savior of the world. Also, they were the first to hear the good news preached to them. Indeed, they were chosen by God to be the people from whom the Messiah came into the world, and they were the most privileged among all people because God first offered salvation to them.

If you accept the understanding of Daniel chapter nine which we just have explained, you will realize that the seventieth week of God's favor upon the Jews was fulfilled almost 2,000 years ago. All seventy weeks (490 years) have passed.

Summary

Look again at Gabriel's initial words of prophecy and see how beautifully they were fulfilled with the coming of Jesus, the Messiah. Gabriel said:

"Seventy weeks have been decreed for your people and your holy city, to finish the transgression, to make an end of sin, to make atonement for iniquity, to bring in everlasting righteousness, to seal up vision and prophecy and to anoint the most holy place." (Dan. 9:24)

The greatest, most wonderful prophecies ever given to the Jews were those pertaining to the coming of Messiah. When Jesus came, the Jews had the opportunity to accept or reject Him. They were given the opportunity *"to finish the transgression, to make an end of sin, to make atonement for iniquity, [and] to bring in everlasting righteousness."* However, they did not recognize Jesus, the Messiah Whom God had promised to send to them.

III. The Jews,
Israel, and the Temple

Issues concerning the future of the Jews are central to our understanding of how the future will unfold. The related topics are seen very differently by those holding to the popular endtime view and those holding to victorious eschatology.

The Jewish Rejection of Messiah

On more than one occasion, Jesus rebuked the Jewish religious leaders for rejecting Him and also for rejecting the prophets and servants whom God had sent to them. For example, our Lord told a parable of a landowner who planted a vineyard, placed it in the care of some vinegrowers, and then went on a journey. When the harvest came, the landowner sent servants to collect the produce but the vinegrowers refused to give it to them. The vinegrowers even beat the landowner's servants and killed one. So the landowner sent another, larger group of servants, and they, too, were beaten and given nothing. Then the landowner sent his own son, for he thought the vinegrowers would respect his son, but even he was abused and then killed by the vinegrowers (Matt. 21:33-46). Matthew 21:45 tells us that the religious leaders heard this parable and knew that Jesus was speaking about them. Jesus confronted them and said:

"Therefore I say to you, the kingdom of God will be taken away from you and given to a people, producing the fruit of it." (Matt. 21:43)

This truth (that the kingdom of God was taken away from the Jewish leaders) is difficult for many Christians today to receive, especially Christians grounded in the popular endtime view, for they are continuing to look for God to restore Israel and use the Jews to bring in the kingdom of God here on Earth.

Jesus went on to tell another parable, speaking of the consequences upon the Jews for their rejection of Him as Messiah. Jesus spoke of a king who invited many honorable people to the wedding feast of his son, but those people all had excuses why they could not attend. After his invitation was rejected a second time, the king became enraged and sent his armies to destroy some of them and to set their city on fire (Matt. 22:7). Jesus explained that the king then invited common people from the streets to the wedding feast of his son, and the people who came in honorable fashion were welcomed by the king to attend that wedding feast (Matt. 22:1-14).

It is in the very next chapter of Matthew where we read about Jesus rebuking the Jewish religious leaders and ending His rebuke by declaring that destruction would come upon Jerusalem and the temple within a generation (Matt. 23:36-38). As we have shown, that was fulfilled in 70 AD. The guilt of all of the righteous blood shed on Earth from the blood of Abel to Zechariah came upon that generation (Matt. 23:35-36). The kingdom of God was taken away from them.

Christians Honoring the Jews

Even though the Jews rejected Jesus as the Messiah, Gentile Christians are to continue honoring them for the sake of their father, Abraham. Even when the Jews were persecuting Christians, Paul explained that Christians must respect the Jews because God chose Abraham and his descendants.

From the standpoint of the gospel they are enemies for your sake, but from the standpoint of God's choice they are beloved for the sake of the fathers.

(Rom. 11:28)

Paul then stated that *"the gifts and calling of God are irrevocable"* (Rom. 11:29), meaning that God called the Jews, and, therefore, they still have a special place in His heart.

Paul further explained this truth using an analogy of an olive tree.

But if some of the branches were broken off, and you, being a wild olive, were grafted in among them and became partaker with them of the rich root of the olive tree, do not be arrogant toward the branches; but if you are arrogant, remember that it is not you who supports the root, but the root supports you.

(Rom. 11:17-18)

115

Gentile Christians may make the mistake of embracing negative attitudes toward the Jews, and, therefore, they need to be reminded that it was the Jews who were entrusted with the Law and the promises of God. They are the ones whom God selected to establish the very foundation of the Christian faith.

For these reasons, Gentile Christians must continue—even today—to honor the Jews.

God has not rejected the natural descendants of Abraham (Rom. 11:1-2, 28-29). Though they rejected Jesus and the kingdom was taken from them, they still have a covenant with God—a unique covenant which assures them a special opportunity in the future. Paul explained in Romans 11:25:

> *...that a partial hardening has happened to Israel until the fullness of the Gentiles has come in.*

From this phrase, "partial hardening," we can expect some Jews to believe in Jesus but the majority will remain in unbelief until the "fullness" or the vast majority of Gentiles are saved.

When God is satisfied with the Gentile harvest, He will open the eyes of the Jews and the vast majority of Jews then will be saved (Rom. 11:23-29). Indeed, there will be a great awakening among the Jews before Jesus Christ returns.

But that won't be the end of the great harvest. The Jews embracing the gospel will bring an even greater awakening amongst the Gentiles. Paul explained this when he wrote that the Jews were hardened for a time in order that the Gentiles might be brought in, but if the Jewish *"...rejection is the reconciliation of the world, what will their acceptance be but life from the dead?"* (Rom 11:15). Indeed, when the Jews get saved it will cause the faith of all to come alive in a way unknown before.

That future awakening will bring unity among Gentile Christians and Jewish Christians. It will be the fulfillment of God's promises to make "one new man," Jews and Gentiles worshipping and serving God together (Eph 2:13-22).

Charles H. Spurgeon
The day shall yet come when the Jews, who were the first apostles to the Gentiles, the first missionaries to us who were afar off, shall be gathered in again. Until that shall be, the fullness of the church's glory can never come. Matchless benefits to the world are bound up with the restoration of Israel; their gathering in shall be as life from the dead. (Vol. 17, 703-4)

What About the Land of Israel?

Prior to 1948, the Jews had almost no governmental authority in the land of Israel since Jerusalem was destroyed in 70 AD. The city was destroyed and the Jews were scattered, exactly as Jesus had prophesied:

> *"And they will fall by the edge of the sword, and will be led captive into all the nations; and Jerusalem will be trampled under foot by the Gentiles until the fullness of the Gentiles are fulfilled."*
>
> (Luke 21:24)

For almost 2,000 years Jerusalem has been trampled under foot by Gentiles. The whole land of Israel has experienced many wars and been under the control of various people groups. It was not until 1948 that Israel became a sovereign nation under the control of Jewish leaders.

Some Christians believe 1948 was the historic fulfillment of God's timetable when Jerusalem no longer would be trampled underfoot and "the fullness of Gentiles" had arrived. Perhaps that date is, indeed, upon us, but there is reason to doubt it because Jerusalem, to some extent, still is being trampled underfoot by non-Jewish people. Though Jews hold the political control, other people groups, and in particular Arabs in that region, battle for control of part or all of that area. In addition, the Muslim temple known as *the Dome of the Rock* stands where the Jewish temple did 2,000 years ago. This being the third most holy site for Muslims across the world, it is an abomination in the sight of Jews.

There also is reason to doubt that the fullness of Gentiles has arrived, because God is continuing to work powerfully among the Gentiles. In fact, there are more Gentiles becoming born-again Christians today than at any time in history (approximately 200,000 per day). The facts do not support the idea that God has shifted His attention from Gentiles to Jews, who for the most part, remain hardened to the gospel, with only a very small percentage believing Jesus is the Messiah.

When, indeed, the fullness of Gentiles arrives, what will happen to the land of Israel?

Those who hold to the popular endtime view believe that at that time God will fulfill His promise of giving the land back to the natural descendants of Abraham. They cite the promise which God made to Abraham many years ago:

> *On that day the Lord made a covenant*
> *with Abram, saying,*
> *"To your descendants I have given this*
> *land,*
> *From the river of Egypt as far as the*
> *great river, the river Euphrates."*
>
> (Gen. 15:18)

Adherents to the popular endtime view believe that God will cause the Jews who have been scattered around the world to migrate back to Israel and establish them as a nation which shall be a light to the world. The Jews will experience God's blessings, and they will be elevated to a position of great authority. Adherents of the victorious view see a very different future for the Jews and Israel. As we already explained, God's 490 years of favor have passed. The Jews will experience a future awakening, but the land will *not* be brought under the exclusive control of the Jews. Please allow us to show you this from Scripture.

First, it is important to point out that God's promise to Abraham was not only for the land which today is known as Israel. God promised all the land from the Nile River in Egypt to the River Euphrates which runs through Syria, Iraq, and Kuwait. This promised land also includes Jordan and parts of Saudi Arabia. If God is going to give the land promised to Abraham to the modern Jews, as popular endtime teachers believe, then the Jews will have to possess all of the land between the two Great Rivers.

Yet, the Bible clearly tells us of the most significant future transformation which will happen in that region. Isaiah prophesied, saying:

> *Thus the Lord will make Himself known to Egypt, and the Egyptians will know the Lord in that day....In that day there will be a highway from Egypt to Assyria, and the Assyrians will come into Egypt and the Egyptians into Assyria, and the*

> *Egyptians will worship with the Assyrians. In that day Israel will be the third party with Egypt and Assyria, a blessing in the midst of the earth, whom the Lord of hosts has blessed, saying, "Blessed is Egypt My people, and Assyria the work of My hands, and Israel My inheritance."*
>
> (Is. 19:21-25)

This passage reveals to us how the day will come when the people of Egypt, Assyria, and Israel will worship the true God. They even will be traveling from one region to another for the purpose of worshipping together.

Isaiah's prophecy sounds almost too good to be true. The people groups he mentioned have battled with each other for generations. Egypt and Assyria lie at the very foundations of the Arab world and a large percentage of Arabs are Muslims. Isaiah said that even Arabs and Jews will be worshipping together.

Isaiah's prophecy also reveals God's heart for Egypt and Assyria, for God called Egypt *"My people"* and Assyria *"the work of My hands."* To hear God speak this way can be difficult for Christians (and Jews) who think of the Jews as God's only chosen ones. Of course, God did choose the Jewish people, but it never was to make them the only humans to receive His favor. Rather, they were chosen as a light to the nations. With the same love that God dealt with the Jews, He always has desired to deal with every people group. He loves the world. The Jews were not the only ones chosen, but they were the first-fruits of the Earth to reveal God's heart to all people.

Jesus told us of a day when He will gather people from outside of the Jews to Himself.

> *"I have other sheep, which are not of this fold; I must bring them also, and they will hear My voice; and they will become one flock with one shepherd."*
>
> (John 10:16)

This is the promise which we are waiting to see fulfilled—one flock consisting of many different people groups.

Where will this happen? All over the world, but most prominently in the Promised Land. God is going to take the most tumultuous region of the world and make it His showcase where different people groups will become one flock with Jesus Christ as their Shepherd.

God is not giving the land which He promised to Abraham exclusively to the Jews. He is going to give it to His children. Paul made this clear when he wrote:

> *Now the promises were spoken to Abraham and to his seed. He does not say, "And to seeds," as referring to many, but rather to one, "And to your seed," that is Jesus Christ.* (Gal. 3:16)

Note this clearly. God did *not* say the promises were

for Abraham and his descendants. They were given by God to Abraham and his descendant—Jesus Christ. Paul further explained how all who put their faith in Jesus will inherit the blessings promised to Abraham.

> *Therefore, be sure that it is those who are of faith who are sons of Abraham.... There is neither Jew nor Greek, there is neither slave nor free man, there is neither male nor female; for you are all one in Christ Jesus. And if you belong to Christ, then you are Abraham's descendants, heirs according to promise.*
>
> (Gal. 3:7-29)

To whom does the Promised Land belong? Who are the heirs? All who put their faith in Jesus Christ.

What then should we expect for the Promised Land? We know that the Jews must have a significant presence there because Isaiah prophesied that the Jews would worship God together with the neighboring countries. However, it also is true that God is giving the land to His children who have been born of the Seed—Jesus. Therefore, we should expect many people groups to settle in that region. As all of those people bow to the Lordship of Jesus Christ, they will be a light to the nations, for that region shall be the most visible place in the Earth where various people groups will come together under one Shepherd, Jesus Christ.

What About the Temple in Jerusalem?

The popular scenario of endtime events assumes that the temple in Jerusalem will be restored before or soon into Daniel's seventieth week. This is necessary since they believe that the antichrist will put an end to the Jewish offerings. According to the Jewish religious system, those offerings must be accompanied by certain religious practices which only can be performed in the temple. Because of this, believers of the popular endtime view eagerly are looking for the temple to be rebuilt.

Those embracing victorious eschatology have very different expectations. The temple was destroyed in 70 AD and God has no intentions of allowing the temple to be rebuilt. Jesus declared to the Jews, *"Behold, your house is being left to you desolate!"* (Matt. 23:38). That temple was meant to be *left* desolate. God does not want to see reconstructed the Jewish religious system which He destroyed. He does not want people to approach Him through animal sacrifices, nor through a high priest in the Jerusalem temple. He does not want that to happen—ever again. Jesus is the only way to the Father.

We can gain further confirmation of this by considering how Jesus and the apostles viewed the temple. The only temple in which they were interested was the new temple of Christians, indwelt by the Holy Spirit. Nowhere can we find any of them making any statement indicating or implying that the temple in Jerusalem ever would be rebuilt. In fact, both Jesus and Stephen were sentenced to death, and central to triggering their deaths were their bold declarations that God did not dwell in stone temples, that the Jewish temple would be destroyed, and a new spiritual temple would be raised (John 2:19; Mark 14:58; Acts 6:13-14, 7:44-50).

The New Testament writers' understanding of the future temple must be key to our understanding of the temple. *Their* understanding must be *our* understanding. We believe that they were inspired by the Holy Spirit, and, therefore, we need to embrace their understanding of how the promises of God would be fulfilled.

Paul talked about the new temple consisting of both Jews and Gentiles being fitly framed together to become a dwelling place for God. That temple, Paul explained, is being built on the foundation of the apostles and prophets, with Jesus Christ as the cornerstone (Eph. 2:11-22). That is the temple which Jesus is building, and the gates of hell shall not prevail against it (Matt. 16:18).

Summary

Some readers may confuse the view which we are presenting with *Replacement Theology*. That would be a mistake. Replacement Theology teaches that God has ended His covenant relationship with the Jews and Christians have replaced the Jews in reference to inheriting all of the promises which were originally made to the Jews. In contrast, we are teaching, *One New Man*, which is the view which sees God keeping His promises and broadening them so they are made available to all who put their faith in Jesus. The ultimate end will be to make Jews and Gentiles into One New Man, worshipping God together (John 10:16; Eph. 2:11-22).

If you embrace the view which we have been explaining, then you will be anticipating a great harvest of souls as the fullness of Gentiles comes in. That harvest will trigger jealousy in the hearts of Jews, who will then respond to the gospel. Then, and only then, will Jews and Gentiles worship Jesus Christ together. Then, and only then, will there be peace in Jerusalem. Let's pray for that day to come quickly.

IV. The Rapture

Both the popular endtime view and victorious eschatology believe in a rapture. Both also believe in the second coming—that Jesus will return in power and glory, appear in the sky, and judge the world.

However, they disagree as to how and when these events will unfold.

Before we explain this difference, it is helpful to point out that the word "rapture" never is used in the Bible. It is an English transliteration of the Latin word *rapio*. That Latin word appears in I Thessalonians 4:17, in the Latin translation of the Bible. The actual Greek word used in this verse is *harpazo*, which is more accurately translated "caught up."

We will use the words "rapture" and "caught up" interchangeably, however, the term "caught up" best conveys the literal meaning intended by the Bible writers.

The Popular Endtime View
Of the Second Coming

The popular endtime view usually depicts the rapture in the following way.

Very soon Jesus will return and secretly appear in the sky, so only believers can see Him. Then all the believers will vanish from planet Earth, being caught up to meet the Lord in the air. Cars will crash as Christian drivers disappear. Piles of clothes will be left behind as Christians vacate this habitation. Also the bodies of dead believers suddenly will vanish from their graves, being taken up to Jesus.

Jesus will take all the believers to heaven for seven years. During that period in heaven, they will be judged regarding their service to God, and then they will receive appropriate rewards. They also will enjoy the marriage banquet of the Lamb, which is the feast of the wedding between Jesus and His Church.

During those seven years, the antichrist will be ruling the world, and most of humanity will follow him. Then there will be a time of tribulation on Earth as God pours out His wrath, destroying much of the Earth including one third of all the people.

Now, here is where it gets a bit confusing: although popular endtime teachers say that the rapture is the second coming of Christ, it only will be part one of the second coming; seven years later, at the end of the heavenly banquet and earthly tribulation, part two of the second coming will take place. Teachers of the popular view say Jesus will return again, bringing all of the believers with Him. This time His return will not be in secret, but rather, every eye will see Him. He will come in judgment and His army will destroy the antichrist at the Battle of Armageddon.

There are slight differences among different popular endtime teachers (i.e., some think the rapture will come half way through the seven years), but this is the most popular version.

Timeline Showing the Popular Endtime View With Two Parts to the Second Coming of Jesus:

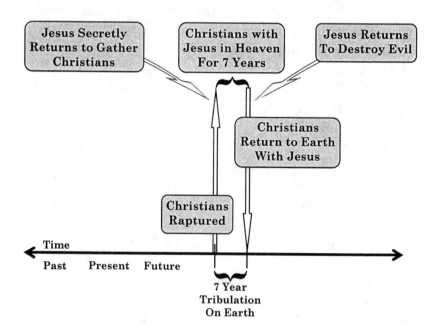

It is worth noting that this view—that the rapture and the return of Jesus to Earth are two different events separated by seven years—was unknown before the late 1850's when a British leader named John Nelson Darby introduced it to his congregation. This teaching became popular after Darby's thoughts were inserted into the footnotes of the *Scofield Reference Bible* in 1909. There is no historical evidence that any group of Christians believed this doctrine before these dates.*

The seven-year period of Christians in heaven is where the popular teachers place Daniel's seventieth week, which we discussed earlier. While the Christians are in heaven, God will give the Jewish people seven years of favor during which time they will be given a place of prominence in world events and government. In the middle of the seven years, popular teachers say that the antichrist will walk into a rebuilt temple in Jerusalem and declare himself as god. At that time, God will pour out His wrath upon the world and a great tribulation shall occur over the whole Earth.

At the end of the seven years, part two of the second coming happens, as Jesus returns to the Earth.

---

* What may be considered an exception to this is the fact that in 1788, a Baptist minister named Morgan Edwards published a book proposing the pre-tribulational rapture, however, the book was not well accepted and quickly went out of print.

The Victorious View of the Second Coming

As we explained earlier, teachers of victorious eschatology believe Daniel's seventieth week happened during the First Century, immediately following the 69 weeks revealed in Daniel chapter nine. Therefore, they do not envision any special seven-year period in the future. They do not see two parts to the second coming of Jesus, separated by seven years. Rather, they see it all happening in one grand event.

Victorious eschatology depicts the rapture in the following way.

Jesus will continue to build His Church, and though Christians will face many trials and setbacks, they will experience more successes than failures. This progressive building will continue until the "Last Day," a day which only God knows. On that day, without any warning signs, Jesus Christ will return in the clouds and every eye will see Him. All believers—living and dead—will be caught up to meet Him as He returns. As they ascend to Jesus, believers will be transformed, their bodies being changed into glorified bodies. Then Jesus will purge the Earth of evil and send the unrighteous to their eternal destiny. He will reward the righteous according to their deeds. This will be the Final Judgment, after which Jesus will descend to the New Earth with all of the Christians to rule and reign forever.

Notice that in this rapture, Christians will not be taken away to heaven for seven years. They will be "caught up," much as a hen would gather her chicks under her wings. Jesus will protect His people while He purges the Earth of evil, then bring the believers down to Earth with Him. For this reason we made the distinction earlier, that the Greek word *harpazo* is more accurately translated "caught up" rather than "caught away." Christians will not be taken away into heaven but they will be caught up to meet the Lord in the air and then descend to Earth to rule and reign with Jesus.*

Victorious Eschatology's View Of the Second Coming:

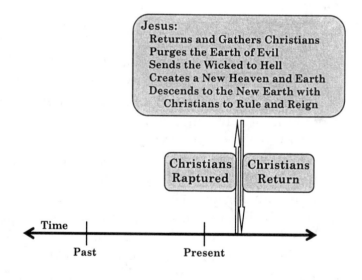

---

* At this point readers trained in eschatology may wonder where we fit the millennial reign of Jesus, and although we do not deal with that subject in this book, there are several good books recommended in Bibliography II, including Harold R. Eberle's *Bringing the Future into Focus.*

When Jesus appears in the sky, His presence will bring an end to sin and an end to history as we know it. The heavens and Earth will go through a metamorphosis, becoming the New Heavens and New Earth. All these things—the resurrection of the dead, the catching up of believers, the return of Christ, the final judgment, and the New Creation—all will happen at the one time, on the same day, the Great and Awesome Day of the Lord.

Please allow us to show you why the victorious view of the rapture is more Scriptural than the popular endtime view.

Examining Key Passages

Although there are a number of passages of Scripture which speak of the return of Christ, there are three main passages (and a controversial fourth passage) that usually are the ones to which are referred when discussing the rapture.

The first two passages speak about Christians receiving glorified bodies:

> *Behold, I tell you a mystery; we will not all sleep, but we will all be changed, in a moment, in the twinkling of an eye, at the last trumpet; for the trumpet will sound, and the dead will be raised imperishable, and we will be changed.* (I Cor. 15:51-52)

> *For our citizenship is in heaven, from which also we eagerly wait for a Savior, the Lord Jesus Christ; who will transform the body of our humble state into conformity with the body of His glory, by the exertion of the power that He has even to subject all things to Himself.*
> (Phil. 3:20-21)

These passages speak about our new bodies and do not deal with the "catching up" aspect of the rapture, and so, they can be used to support either the popular endtime view or victorious eschatology.

A third passage used to teach about the rapture is I Thessalonians 4:16-17:

> *For the Lord Himself will descend from heaven with a shout, with the voice of the archangel and with the trumpet of God, and the dead in Christ will rise first. Then we who are alive and remain will be caught up together with them in the clouds to meet the Lord in the air, and so we shall always be with the Lord.*
>
> (I Thes. 4:16-17)

This is the key passage. It is the only one which speaks of us being "caught up" to meet the Lord in the air. As we noted earlier, it does not say we will be "caught away" to heaven for seven years. It says we will be "caught up" to meet the Lord in the air.

Teachers of victorious eschatology will compare this catching up with people going to meet a friend who just arrived at the local airport. When he arrives, his friends may come to meet him. They will not fly away with him in another airplane, but they will accompany him as he comes to their home. In similar fashion, Jesus is returning, not to take believers away, but to be with them on Earth. Christians will meet Him in the air, and they will hesitate in that place only for as long as it takes for Jesus to purge the Earth of evil—a process which will be instantaneous, or almost so, because His glorious appearing will transform everything.

Earlier, we said that there was a fourth passage of

Scripture usually discussed in connection with the rapture, and that this was a controversial passage. In fact, most scholars who teach the popular endtime view readily admit that this passage is used wrongfully by the more popular "science-fiction" type of endtime teachers and novelists. It is the famous "Left Behind" passage in Matthew 24:

> *"But of that day and hour no one knows, not even the angels in heaven, nor the Son, but the Father alone. For the coming of the Son of Man will be just as the days of Noah. For as in those days before the flood, they were eating and drinking, marrying and giving in marriage, until the day that Noah entered the ark, and they did not understand until the flood came and took them all away; so will the coming of the Son of Man be. Then there will be two men in the field; one will be taken and one will be left. Two women will be grinding at the mill; one will be taken and one will be left. Therefore be on the alert, for you do not know which day your Lord is coming."*
>
> (Matt. 24:36-42)

Earlier, when we discussed Matthew 24, we explained how this passage is not talking about a rapture of Christians, but the Final Great Day of Judgment.

To confirm this, we can note that the ones who are

seen taken away in this passage are not believers, as popular endtime teachers say. Jesus is saying just the opposite. In Noah's day judgment came suddenly and swept the ungodly away. Noah and his family were left behind to inherit the Earth. If we apply this as Jesus is to the Final Great Day of Judgment, then we will see the ungodly being swept away in judgment, while the righteous are left behind to rule and reign on Earth.

This is exactly what Jesus had taught His disciples in Matthew 13, in the parable of the wheat and tares. He tells the parable in verses 24-30, and then in verses 36-43, He gives His disciples the explanation of the parable.

> *"The one who sows the good seed is the Son of Man, and the field is the world; and as for the good seed, these are the sons of the kingdom; and the tares are the sons of the evil one; and the enemy who sowed them is the devil, and the harvest is the end of the age; and the reapers are angels."* (Matt. 13:37b-39)

After giving this quick overview of how time will progress, Jesus focused on the end when He will return for judgment:

> *"So just as the tares are gathered up and burned with fire, so shall it be at the end of the age. The Son of Man will send forth His angels, and they will gather out*

*of His kingdom all stumbling blocks, and
those who commit lawlessness, and will
throw them into the furnace of fire; in
that place there will be weeping and
gnashing of teeth. Then the righteous
will shine forth as the sun in the kingdom of their Father."* (Matt. 13:40-43a)

Jesus is very clear. It is the ungodly who will be removed, gathered, taken. It is the righteous who will
be left behind to shine as the sun.

Summary

If you embrace the victorious understanding of the second coming of Jesus, you will not see it happening in two parts. You will see that there is no seven-year period during which Christians are in heaven while the wrath of God is poured out on the Earth. When Jesus returns, He actually and literally will return to the New Earth.

Another major difference between the popular endtime view and victorious eschatology is the focus on what will happen in the near future. The popular teachers emphasize the coming rapture so much that it remains on the forefront of the listeners' minds; it is the next great event to which they eagerly are looking forward. In contrast, Christians who embrace victorious eschatology believe in a coming rapture, but their main focus is on the Church arising in glory and a great harvest of souls across the world. Most popular teachers also will say that they are looking for a great harvest, but it is not their *primary* hope. They still believe that the world is going to get worse and worse, the antichrist will take over, and Jesus will rapture them away while God pours out His wrath on the Earth. Hence, the popular teachers are ever conscious of their soon-coming escape by way of the rapture, and the adherents of victorious eschatology are most conscious of the coming great harvest.

V. The Endtimes

The following terms are used interchangeably:

endtimes
end days
last days
latter days

Since the plural form is used in each of these, we can gather that the related events will not happen in a single day, but will extend over a period of time.

When the Bible speaks of *the day*, in its singular form, it usually is referring to the Final Great Judgment Day in which all people will be gathered before the Lord for judgment. *The day* or what is also called *the day of the Lord* will be the climax of history and should be distinguished from *the endtimes*.

In the discussion to follow, we will not be talking about *the day of the Lord*, but we will examine the Bible's use of *endtimes, end days, last days, and latter days.*

The Apostles Believed
They Were in the Endtimes

Several Bible passages reveal to us that the First-Century apostles believed they were living in the end-times. For example, when Peter preached on Pentecost day, he quoted from the book of Joel applying the term "last days" to the experience of the Holy Spirit being poured out at that time in their lives.

> *"For these men are not drunk, as you*
>   *suppose...*
> *but this is what was spoken of through*
>   *the prophet Joel:*
> *'And it shall be in the last days,' God*
>   *says,*
> *'That I will pour forth of My Spirit on all*
>   *mankind....' "*
>   (Acts 2:15-17; underlining added)

Peter was convinced that he was living in the last days, and he was so confident of this that he quoted a passage from Joel declaring that it was fulfilled on the day of Pentecost.

Peter also wrote in his first epistle with the understanding that he was living in the last times:

> *For He was foreknown before the founda-*
> *tions of the world, but has appeared in*
> *these last times for the sake of you....*
>   (I Peter 1:20; underlining added)

Note how Peter defined the *last times* as the times in which Jesus appeared to them during their lifetimes.

Paul also spoke in such terms as he explained how we should learn from the events which happened in the Old Testament:

> *Now these things happened to them as an example, and they were written for our instruction, upon whom the ends of the ages have come.*
>
> (I Cor. 10:11, underlining added)

Was Paul wrong? Was Peter wrong? Were they confused?

If we study the teachings of other New-Testament writers, we learn that they, too, believed they were living in the last days.

The writer of Hebrews wrote:

> *God, after He spoke long ago to the fathers in the prophets in many portions and in many ways, in these last days has spoken to us in His Son....*
>
> (Heb. 1:1-2; underlining added)

The writer was convinced that he was living in the last days, and he defined the last days as the period during which God spoke through Jesus while Jesus was alive on Earth.

We see that James had the same belief when we read how he rebuked some greedy rich people, telling them of the destruction about to come upon them, saying:

> *It is in the last days that you have stored*
> *up your treasure!*
>   (James 5:3; underlining added)

James believed that the "last days" was then, at that time in history during the First Century.

The apostle John stated this belief with just as much conviction:

> *Children, it is the last hour; and just as*
> *you heard that antichrist is coming, even*
> *now many antichrists have appeared;*
> *from this we know it is the last hour.*
>   (I John 2:18; underlining added)

John was convinced that he was living in the last hour, based on the presence of antichrists. John expected his disciples to realize this, too.

Were the New-Testament writers wrong? Did they live in the endtimes? Or are the endtimes coming in our future? Did the apostles miss it by 2,000 years?

The Popular Endtime View Of the Endtimes

A major point of the popular endtime teachers is that we—living 2,000 years after the First-Century apostles—are in the last days, or at least approaching very closely to those days. When they talk about the last days or endtimes, they are referring to the scenario of events which they believe will culminate in the second coming of Jesus. Whenever the popular endtime teachers speak of the rapture, great tribulation, the antichrist, and the end of the world, they are referring to this endtime period. They also speak of "signs" of the endtimes, including earthquakes, famines, disasters, and people falling away from the faith. All these things are discussed in the context of the endtimes as a period which will come in the near future or perhaps recently has begun.

Timeline Showing the Endtimes
According to the Popular Endtime View:

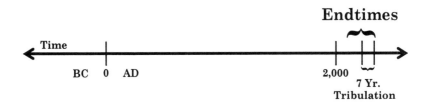

If a popular endtime teacher is pressed on the point that the New-Testament writers believed they were in the last days, the popular teacher will concede, and then say that the apostles missed it, or they will say that the endtimes is the period from the resurrection of Jesus to the end of the world. They will say that the last days has extended more than 2,000 years. Though they make this adjustment in their definition of the endtimes when necessary, they quickly will return to their discussions about the endtimes being the few short years right before the end of the world.

The Victorious View
Of the Endtimes

Teachers holding to victorious eschatology do not jump back and forth between two different definitions of endtimes. They believe the words of the New-Testament writers literally. Peter, Paul, James, and John were not wrong. The apostles were living in the last days. *We* do *not* live in the endtimes.

Please, allow us to explain.

First, we need to define what the Bible meant by the endtimes or last days.

Joel defined the *last days* as the period in which the Holy Spirit would be poured out on the world. Peter accepted Joel's definition and believed that it was fulfilled on Pentecost Day (Acts 2:16-17).

Peter also identified the *last days* as the period during which Jesus walked on Earth (I Peter 1:20).

James understood the *last days* to be in his lifetime, when destruction was about to come upon his generation (James 5:3).

John defined the *last hour* as the period during which antichrists were active, and John believed those antichrists were active then (I John 2:18).

The writer of Hebrews used the terminology *last days* to refer to the period in which God spoke to humanity through Jesus Christ while Jesus was alive on Earth 2,000 years ago (Heb. 1:1-2).

According to every one of these definitions of "endtimes," the apostles did live in the endtimes.

If we believe that the Bible writers were inspired

by God to write what they wrote, then we cannot say that they missed it. For example, John emphatically said, *"it is the last hour"* (I John 2:18). Since we believe that God inspired John, we have to conclude that God believed—knew—it was the last hour 2,000 years ago.

Teachers of victorious eschatology agree with what the Bible clearly says. The endtimes took place during the First Century.

Timeline Showing the Endtimes According to Victorious Eschatology:

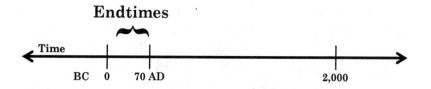

How could it be possible that the period called the endtimes was in the First Century?

Put yourselves in the shoes of the Jewish people in the days of Jesus. Those who knew their Scriptures—the Old Testament—knew the promises of God. The most hopeful promises centered on a coming Messiah, a New Kingdom, and God making a New Covenant with His people. Devout Jews centered their lives around these promises. So important were these promises that they were always looking for the days promised to them by the Old-Testament prophets.

When Jesus came, He brought in the New Kingdom. He established the New Covenant. The temple was destroyed. The old religious system ended. The end of the old came in the First Century. That was the endtimes. It ended the old. The endtimes was the period in which God abolished the old by establishing the new. It went from the day Jesus revealed Himself as Messiah to the destruction of the temple in Jerusalem in 70 AD. The apostles were not wrong. They did live in the endtimes.

We live in new times! In a new covenant and in a new kingdom!

This understanding can be shocking and unsettling when first heard by Christians trained under popular endtime teaching. They have heard the terms *endtimes* and *last days* used so many times in reference to the end of the world that they cannot conceive of so great an error in their thinking. Yet, there is *no* Scripture which supports the view that the endtimes are in our future. *Every place* the terminology is used in the Bible, it refers to the time in the First Century when the old was put away and God fulfilled His promises to establish a New Covenant.

This issue is important not only for Christians, but also for our defense of the faith before non-Christians. One of the most influential atheists of modern times was a scholar named Bertrand Russell. In his book, *Why I Am Not a Christian,* Russell points out how wrong and misled the disciples were by believing that they were living in endtimes.* More importantly, Russell declared that Jesus was a false

---

* Bertrand Russell, *Why I Am Not a Christian: And other Essays on Religion and Related Topics,* ed. Paul Edwards (London: Allen & Unwin / New York:Simon & Schuster, 1957), p. vi.

prophet, since the events of Matthew 24 (at least to his understanding) did not happen within a generation. Russell and many other influential atheists have ridiculed Christianity, pointing out how wrong Jesus and the disciples were to believe that they were living in the endtimes.

Instead of making excuses for our Lord and the disciples, let's believe them. Let's accept the fact that *they did live in the endtimes,* and we do not.

If we shift our understanding of the endtimes from being in our future to our past, we also will change our expectations of the future spiritual and moral conditions of the Church and the world. You see, there is one Bible passage which tells us that in latter days many will fall away from the faith (I Tim. 4:1-3; quoted below). Then there is another passage which talks about evil people increasing in the last times (Jude 1:18; quoted below).

Since popular endtime teaching maintains that the latter days are coming in our future, before the end of the world, they teach from these two Bible passages that the world is going to get worse and worse, spiritually and morally.

In reality, the Bible writers were *not* talking about *our future*, but the endtimes in which they were living, which is evident when we read the context in which they wrote. Paul wrote to Timothy:

> But the Spirit explicitly says that <u>in later times</u> some will fall away from the faith, paying attention to deceitful spirits and doctrines of demons....
>
> (I Tim. 4:1-3; underlining added)

Paul wrote these words in the context of explaining the actions of evil people right around Timothy at that time. Paul was exhorting Timothy that *he* should not be surprised at the evil *around him,* for indeed,

159

the Holy Spirit had revealed to them that such things would happen in latter times. Paul was assuming that he and Timothy were living in those latter times.

Jude wrote similarly in his letter explaining that the evil people which they were facing should be expected since the apostles had warned about the evil people who would come in the last times.

> *"In the last time there will be mockers, following after their own ungodly lusts."*
> (Jude 1:18; underlining added)

Jude was not talking about mockers to come 2,000 years later. In the context, he was referring to the mockers living in his day with which he was having to deal.

This makes perfect sense when we recognize the terrible spiritual and moral conditions of the people under the rule of Rome during the First Century. Even the Jewish people were known for their depravity. The Jewish historian Josephus described the conditions of his own people, that is, the generation which witnessed the destruction of Jerusalem:

> ...neither did any other city ever suffer such miseries, nor did any age ever breed a generation more fruitful in wickedness that this was, from the beginning of the world. (v:x:5)

Add to this picture, the cruel persecutions which were going on, with Christians being tortured and killed by

Jews and Romans. Also, many people were being taken in by false messiahs, prophets, and teachers. That was a terribly deceived and corrupt generation.

If we recognize the spiritual and moral conditions of the time we easily can understand the two New Testament passages which warn of mockers and evil people during the endtimes. When we study the contexts of both passages we cannot deny that the authors were talking about evil people active in the First Century.

This understanding is important because it disarms popular endtime teachers who misuse these two Bible passages to say that evil will get worse and worse as we approach the return of Jesus Christ.

Teachers of victorious eschatology do not have a negative view of the future or the world. They believe that we live in the new times and in these new days the Church is being raised to a position of unity, maturity, and glory. Furthermore, the Kingdom of God will continue to grow until it fills the Earth.*

---

* In some contexts, teachers of victorious eschatology may use the terms *endtimes* or *last days* to refer to the future period during which Jesus returns. However, they do not confuse that future reference with how the terminology is used in the Bible to refer to the First-Century transition from old to new.

Conclusion

This book may leave some unanswered questions in the minds of readers who never before have been exposed to victorious eschatology. In a work of this length we cannot deal with the book of Revelation, the man of lawlessness in Thessalonians, nor all of the Old Testament prophecies concerning the endtimes or the end of the world. We can assure you that there are victorious ways of understanding each and every passage, and we have listed in the bibliography books which offer those views.

We are not concerned that you understand every Bible passage the way we do. In fact, we realize that many scholarly teachers holding to victorious eschatology explain various verses in slightly different ways than we have. However, our primary concern is that you embrace a victorious view.

A victorious view will inspire you to plan for the future, move ahead with courage, invest in the next generation, and believe God for greater things yet to come.

Satan is not taking over this world. Jesus Christ is Lord, and He will rule until every enemy is put under His feet.

Bibliography I

The books listed below are those from which direct quotations are made or which have been used as references in gathering material for this book.

Athanasius, St. *On the Incarnation*. Translated and edited by Sister Penelope Lawson, S.C.M.V. New York: Macmillan Publishing Co., 1946.

Aquinas, Thomas. *Golden Chain*. New York: Mowbray, 1956.

Bray, John. *Matthew 24 Fulfilled*. Lakeland, FL: John Bray, 1996.

Calvin, John. *Calvin's Commentaries*. Reprinted 1984, Grand Rapids, MI: Baker Book House, 1847.

Calvin, John. *Commentary on the Harmony of the Evangelists, Matthew, Mark, and Luke*. Translated by William Pringle, Grand Rapids, MI: Eerdmans, 1949.

Chilton, David. *Paradise Restored*. Tyler, TX: Dominion Press, 1999.

Currie, David. *Rapture, The Endtimes Error that Leaves the Bible Behind*. Manchester, New Hampshire: Sophia Institute Press, 2003.

Edwards, Jonathan. *The Works of Jonathan Edwards.* Edited by Edward Hickman. 2 volumes. 1834. Reprinted. Edinburgh: Banner of Truth, 1974.

Eusebius, Pamphilius. *Ecclesiastical History* (325). Translated by Kirsopp Lake, New York: Harvard University Press, 1980.

Eusebius, Pamphilius. *The History of the Church.* New York: Dorset Press, Edition of 1965.

Eusebius, Pamphilius. *The Proof of the Gospel* (c. 300). Translated by W.J. Ferrar, New York: The Macmillan Co., 1920.

Josephus, Flavius. *Josephus, The Complete Works.* Translated by William Whiston, Nashville, TN: Thomas Nelson Publishers, 1998.

Kik, J. Marcellus. *An Eschatology of Victory.* Nutley, NJ: Presbyterian and Reformed Publishing Co., 1971.

Mauro, Philip, *The Seventy Weeks and the Great Tribulation.* Clackamas, OR: Emissary Publications.

Pike, G.H. *Life and Work of Charles Haddon Spurgeon.* Edinburgh, UK: Funk and Wagnalls Co., 1992.

Origen, *Origen Against Celsus.* Translated by James Bellanmy, London: B. Mills and J. Robinson, 1660.

Sproul, R. C. *The Last Days According to Jesus.* Grand Rapids, MI: Baker Books, 1998.

Spurgeon, Charles. *Commentary on Matthew.* Grand Rapids, MI: Fleming H Revell Co., 1987.

Spurgeon, Charles. *The Gospel of the Kingdom.* Pasadena, TX: Pilgrim Publications, 1974.

The Ante-Nicene Fathers: Translation of the Fathers Down to A.D. 325. 10 volumes. Edited by Alexander Roberts and James Donaldson, Grand Rapids, MI: Eerdmans Publishing Co., 1989.

Wesley, John. *The Works of John Wesley.* Edited by Albert C. Outler, Nashville: Abingdon, 1985.

Bibliography II

Although we do not endorse everything taught in the following books (some offer the full preterist view and others the partial preterist view), each author will broaden your understanding of victorious eschatology.

Bray, John. *Matthew 24 Fulfilled.* Lakeland, FL: John Bray, 1996.

Chilton, David. *Paradise Restored.* Tyler, TX: Dominion Press, 1999.

Currie, David. *Rapture, The Endtimes Error that Leaves the Bible Behind.* Manchester, NH: Sophia Institute Press, 2003.

De Mar, Gary. *Last Days Madness: Obsession of the Modern Church.* 3rd ed. Atlanta: American Vision, 1997.

Eberle, Harold R. *Bringing the Future into Focus.* Yakima, WA: Worldcast Publishing, 2002.

Hamon, Bill. *The Eternal Church.* Point Washington, FL: Christian International Publishers, 1981.

Josephus, Flavius. *Josephus, The Complete Works.* Translated by William Whiston, Nashville, TN: Thomas Nelson Publishers, 1998.

Kik, J. Marcellus. *An Eschatology of Victory*. Nutley, NJ: Presbyterian and Reformed Publishing Co., 1971.

Mauro, Philip, *The Seventy Weeks and the Great Tribulation*. Clackamas, OR: Emissary Publications.

Murray, Iain H. *The Puritan Hope*. Carlisle, PA: The Banner of Truth Trust, 1998.

Noe, John. *Shattering the Left Behind Delusion*. Bradford, PA: International Preterist Association. 2000.

Sproul, R. C. *The Last Days According to Jesus*. Grand Rapids, MI: Baker Books, 1998.

Other Books by Harold R. Eberle

THE COMPLETE WINESKIN (Fourth edition)

The Body of Christ is in a reformation. God is pouring out the Holy
Spirit and our wineskins must be changed to handle the new wine.
Will the Church come together in unity? Where do small group
meetings fit? How does the anointing of God work and what is your
role? What is the 5-fold ministry? How are apostles, prophets,
evangelists, pastors and teachers going to rise up and work together?
This book puts into words what you have been sensing in your spirit.
(Eberle's best seller, translated into many languages, distributed
worldwide.)

TWO BECOME ONE (Second edition)

*Releasing God's Power for Romance, Sexual Freedom
and Blessings in Marriage*

Kindle afresh the "buzz of love." Find out how to make God's law
of binding forces work for you instead of against you. The keys to a
thrilling, passionate, and fulfilling marriage can be yours if you
want them. This book is of great benefit to pastors, counselors,
young singles, divorcees and especially married people. Couples
are encouraged to read it together.

GOD'S LEADERS FOR TOMORROW'S WORLD

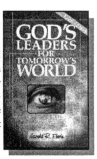

(Revised/expanded edition) You sense a call to leadership in your life,
but questions persist: "Does God want me to rise up? Is this pride? Do I
truly know where to lead? How can I influence people?" Through a
new understanding of leadership dynamics, learn how to develop godly
charisma. Confusion will melt into order when you see the God-
ordained lines of authority. Fear of leadership will change to confidence
as you learn to handle power struggles. Move into your "metron," that
is, your God-given authority. You can be all God created you to be!

BRINGING THE FUTURE INTO FOCUS

An Introduction to the Progressive Christian Worldview

What does the future hold? Will there be peace or war? Are the
people of God going to rise up in glory and unity or will they be
overcome by apathy and deception? Is Jesus coming for a spotless
Bride or is He going to rescue a tattered band of zealots out of a
wicked chaotic mess? Where is God taking humanity in the Twenty-
First Century?
This book will answer your questions and fill you with hope.

Other Books by Harold R. Eberle

JESUS CAME OUT OF THE TOMB...SO CAN YOU!
A Brief Explanation of Resurrection-based Christianity
In our sincere attempts to please God and rid ourselves of sin, we continually focus on the single event which traditional theology tells us paid for our sins. Yet we rarely experience the fullness of God's promises. If God raised Jesus from the tomb in power and glory, why aren't we living in that resurrection? If God raised Jesus into heaven, and us with Him, why aren't we experiencing His victory? We can!

YOU SHALL RECEIVE POWER
God's Spirit will fill you in measures beyond what you are experiencing presently. This is not just about Pentecostal or Charismatic blessings. There is something greater. It is for all Christians, and it will build a bridge between those Christians who speak in tongues and those who do not. It is time for the whole Church to take a fresh look at the work of the Holy Spirit in our individual lives. This book will help you. It will challenge you, broaden your perspective, set you rejoicing, fill you with hope, and leave you longing for more of God.

RELEASING KINGS
INTO THE MARKETPLACE FOR MINISTRY
Co-authored by John Garfield and Harold R. Eberle.
This books explains how marketplace ministry will operate in concert with local churches and pastors. It provides a Scriptural basis for the expansion of the Kingdom of God into all areas of society. It paints a picture of Kings who are naturally competitive, creative, and decisive, who are being used to fulfill the Great Commission.

DEVELOPING A PROSPEROUS SOUL
VOL I: HOW TO OVERCOME A POVERTY MIND-SET
VOL II: HOW TO MOVE INTO GOD'S FINANCIAL BLESSINGS

There are fundamental changes you can make in the way you think which will help release God's blessings. This is a balanced look at the promises of God with practical steps you can take to move into financial freedom. It is time for Christians to recapture the financial arena. These two volumes will inspire and create faith in you to fulfill God's purposes for your life.

Other Books by Harold R. Eberle

IF GOD IS GOOD,
WHY IS THERE SO MUCH SUFFERING AND PAIN?

Life isn't fair! Terrorist bombings. Ethnic cleansing. Body-ravaging diseases. Murder. Child abuse. Natural disasters. Genetic maladies. These travesties, global and seemingly relentless, drive us to the limits of our reasoning. When pain and suffering invade our well-laid plans for a good life, we ask the gut question: Why, God, why? In this book, Harold R. Eberle evaluates the role God plays in the Earth, explores the origin of suffering, and reassures us of God kind intentions toward us.

GRACE...THE POWER TO REIGN

The Light Shining from Romans 5-8

We struggle against sin and yearn for God's highest. Yet, on a bad day it is as as if we are fighting with gravity. Questions go unanswered:

• Where is the power to overcome temptations and trials?

• Is God really willing to breathe into us so that these dry bones can live and we may stand strong?

For anyone who ever has clenched his fist in the struggle to live godly, here are the answers.

THE SPIRITUAL, MYSTICAL, AND SUPERNATURAL

The first five volumes of Harold R. Eberle's series of books entitled, *Spiritual Realities,* have been condensed into this one volume, 372 pages in length. Topics are addressed such as how the spiritual and natural worlds are related, angelic and demonic manifestations, signs and wonders, miracles and healings, the anointing, good versus evil spiritual practices, how people are created by God to access the spiritual realm, how the spirits of people interact, how people sense things in the spirit realm, and much more.

Individual volumes of the *Spiritual Realities* series are available also.

To place an order or to check current prices call:
1-800-308-5837 within the USA or:
509-248-5837 from outside the USA

Worldcast Publishing
P.O. Box 10653
Yakima, WA 98909-1653

E-mail: office@worldcastpublishing.com
Web Site: www.worldcastpublishing.com